Enchantment of America

ALABAMA

By Allan Carpenter

CHILDRENS PRESS, CHICAGO

ACKNOWLEDGMENTS

For advice and assistance in the preparation of the revised edition, the author wishes to thank:
RAWDON BARNES, Director, Public Relations, Alabama Development Office and
SARA G. REDDING, Bureau of Publicity and Information, State of Alabama

American Airlines—Anne Vitaliano, Director of Public Relations; *Capitol Historical Society*, Washington, D. C.; *Newberry Library*, Chicago, Dr. Lawrence Towner, Director; *Northwestern University Library*, Evanston, Illinois; *United Airlines*—John P. Grember, Manager of Special Promotions; Joseph P. Hopkins, Manager, News Bureau.

UNITED STATES GOVERNMENT AGENCIES: *Department of Agriculture*—Robert Hailstock, Jr., Photography Division, Office of Communication; Donald C. Schuhart, Information Division, Soil Conservation Service. *Army*—Doran Topolosky, Public Affairs Office, Chief of Engineers, Corps of Engineers. *Department of Interior*—Louis Churchville, Director of Communications; EROS Space Program—Phillis Wiepking, Community Affairs; Charles Withington, Geologist; Mrs. Ruth Herbert, Information Specialist; Bureau of Reclamation; National Park Service—Fred Bell and the individual sites; Fish and Wildlife Service—Bob Hines, Public Affairs Office. *Library of Congress*—Dr. Alan Fern, Director of the Department of Research; Sara Wallace, Director of Publications; Dr. Walter W. Ristow, Chief, Geography and Map Division; Herbert Sandborn, Exhibits Officer. *National Archives*—Dr. James B. Rhoads, Archivist of the United States; Albert Meisel, Assistant Archivist for Educational Programs; David Eggenberger, Publications Director; Bill Leary, Still Picture Reference; James Moore, Audio-Visual Archives. *United States Postal Service*—Herb Harris, Stamps Division.

For advice, counsel, and gracious help in the first edition, the author thanks:
Consultant Dr. Charles G. Summersell, Head, History Department, University of Alabama; Albert Burton Moore, Graduate Dean Emeritus, University of Alabama; Richard Hail Brown, Birmingham; Bureau of Publicity and Information, State of Alabama; Alabama State Chamber of Commerce; Mobile Area Chamber of Commerce.

Cover photograph: Alabama garden scene
Pages 2-3: Bellingrath Gardens, Allan Carpenter
Page 3: (Map) USDI Geological Survey
Pages 4-5: Mobile Bay area, EROS Space Photo, USDI Geological Survey, EROS Data Center

Project Editor, Revised Edition:
Joan Downing
Assistant Editor, Revised Edition:
Mary Reidy

Library of Congress
Cataloging in Publication Data

Carpenter, John Allan, 1917-
Alabama.

(Enchantment of America)
Includes index.
SUMMARY: Discusses the history, geography, resources, famous citizens, and points of interest of the state known as the Heart of Dixie.
1. Alabama—Juvenile literature.
[1. Alabama] I. Title
F326.3.C3   1978   976.1   77-13920
ISBN 0-516-04101-0

Contents

The hatred of the Indians for the persecutions by de Soto and his men was so great that the Spanish never were able to realize their later ambition to colonize the southeastern United States. One of the few Spaniards who spoke out against his countrymen's cruelty to the Indians was Bartolome de Las Casas. This rare illustration of the massacre at Cholula is one of the watercolors he painted for his book, Destruction of the Indies.

A True Story to Set the Scene

KING TASCALUSA'S REVENGE

Hernando de Soto was governor of Cuba and adelantado of Florida, which his ruler, the king of Spain, claimed included all of what is now the southeast United States. For several years de Soto had been exploring this territory, leading a great expedition of six hundred men, two hundred horses, large herds of cattle, mules, and hogs, and great quantities of supplies.

For protection as he rode about the country, de Soto took Indian chiefs captive and held them as hostages so that their people would not attack. He made them provide hundreds of men and women to serve as baggage carriers and servants; most of them were forced to shuffle along in chains as slaves.

The fantastic expedition entered what is now Alabama from present-day Tennessee. They followed the rivers south through the state. De Soto learned that the greatest leader of the region, possibly the most powerful monarch in all of North America at that time, was King Tascalusa of the Mobilian tribe. Tascalusa and de Soto had been in touch by messenger before they met.

De Soto was a small man with a dark beard and flashing eyes. King Tascalusa was over seven feet (about two meters) tall.

When the two met on October 10, 1540, Tascalusa, whose name meant Black Warrior, welcomed de Soto as a brother. He knew, however, of the great tragedies de Soto had brought to other tribes.

As Tascalusa rose to leave the meeting, de Soto insisted that he remain. De Soto demanded hundreds of Tascalusa's subjects for burden bearers and a hundred women as servants.

Tascalusa informed de Soto that his demands for men would be met, but he would have to wait for the women until they could reach the town of Mabila, about 75 miles (nearly 121 kilometers) down the twisting Alabama River. Tascalusa hurriedly sent messengers to Mabila to prepare the defenses for their coming.

Mabila was a strongly fortified town, protected by walls formed of heavy vertical tree trunks, reinforced with horizontal logs, and packed solid with dirt or clay. Every fifty feet (about fifteen meters) along the walls were watchtowers for archers. The houses were big and sturdy. There were about eighty houses. In each there were five hundred to fifteen hundred people.

When the party reached the walls, most of de Soto's men were required to stay outside the town. Tascalusa soon gave the signal to attack. The Spaniards who were inside were quickly driven outside the walls, but the Indians made the mistake of following them from the town.

The Indians used tremendous bows, so heavy that none of the Spaniards were able to draw them. A large number of the Spaniards wore armor, so the arrows did little damage. The Spaniards carried crossbows, swords, battleaxes, and clumsy guns known as harque-busses. But it was the horses of the cavalry that terrorized the Indians, because horses were not known in that region.

The battle raged on, and de Soto's main force joined the fight. Although the Indians fought bravely and well, the Spaniards managed to knock down the doors of Mabila. They swarmed in, set fire to the houses and eventually slaughtered all the Indian men. The last brave left alive climbed a tree, took the leather thong from his bow, and hanged himself.

The fate of King Tascalusa is unknown. Many historians have said that he died with his men.

The Battle of Mabila was one of the bloodiest of all Indian battles. About twenty-five hundred Indians and twenty-two Spaniards were killed. Twenty-nine Spaniards were wounded, including de Soto.

After waiting about a month for the wounded to recover, de Soto returned to the interior where he contracted a fever and died.

Due to the failure of de Soto's grandiose scheme, the Spaniards did little about colonizing the rich southeast until it was too late, and they were driven out. If de Soto had treated the Indians with kindness and respect, the Spanish probably would have won the Indians' friendship and laid the foundation for a great empire.

Because this did not happen, it has been said that the great King Tascalusa eventually proved to be the true winner of the tragic Battle of Mabila, gaining his long-delayed revenge on future generations of de Soto's countrymen.

Lay of the Land

VEGETATION GATHERERS

There is a persistent error concerning the name of Alabama. When early Indian tribes first saw the land we call Alabama, they were so impressed, according to some historians, that they promptly cried out, "Alba amo!" which freely translated means "This is a goodly land. Here we rest." From those Indian words, many books say, comes the state's name of Alabama. This is now considered incorrect. Alabama was the Indian word meaning "clearers of thickets" or "vegetation gatherers."

Alabama as we know it today is bounded on the north by Tennessee, on the east by Georgia, on the south by Florida and the Gulf of Mexico; its long western border touches only Mississippi.

Alabama's total area of 51,609 square miles (133,667 square kilometers) is divided into four major regions—the 17,000 square mile (44,030 square kilometer) coastal alluvial plain to the south, Cumberland Plateau on the north, and the Coosa Valley, which is almost hemmed in by the fourth region, the Piedmont Plateau.

FACE WITH DISTINCTIVE FEATURES

Probably the most distinctive feature of Alabama is its network of rivers with their musical and romantic sounding names.

There are two principal drainage systems. The Tennessee River wanders from east to west across the northern part of the state. Waters from this drainage system reach the Gulf of Mexico in a roundabout way via the Ohio and Mississippi rivers.

A divide separates the waters of the Tennessee from those of the vast Mobile-Tensaw river system which flows to the south.

The great Chattahoochee River forms part of the eastern boundary, but very little of the water it drains comes from Alabama.

In addition to the Tennessee, the main internal rivers of Alabama are the Tombigbee and the Alabama. The Alabama River is formed where the Coosa and Tallapoosa meet just north of Montgomery. A

Noccalula Falls

principal tributary is the Cahaba River. Main tributaries of the Tombigbee are the Black Warrior River and the Sipsey River. This should not to be confused with the Sipsey Fork of the Black Warrior.

The junction of the Tombigbee and Alabama rivers forms one of the most complicated river systems in the country. Below this point the Tombigbee is known as the Mobile River, and the Alabama River is called the Tensaw River. The Mobile and Tensaw are joined at several points by crisscrossing of bayous and channels until they reach Mobile Bay. At this point sizeable deltas are formed.

The southeast corner of Alabama is drained by smaller independent river systems—the Conecuh with its tributary the Sepulga, and the Choctawhatchee, fed by the Pea River.

The long thin peninsula of Mobile Point and the equally long and thin Dauphin Island appear to be two doors guarding the entrance of magnificent Mobile Bay—one of the best natural harbors of the country.

Most of Alabama's lakes have been made by damming large rivers. The part of the Tennessee River in Alabama is now almost a chain of lakes, with Pickwick Lake and Wilson Lake formed by Wilson Dam; enormous Wheeler Lake, a product of Wheeler Dam; and Guntersville Lake, backed up by Guntersville Dam almost to the Tennessee line.

Demopolis Dam was completed in 1962, and the waters of both the Tombigbee and Black Warrior rivers flooded into huge lakes. Not far from Birmingham are Lake Bankhead on the Black Warrior and Smith Reservoir on the Sipsey branch.

The Coosa River has Jordan Lake, Lake Mitchell, and Weiss Reservoir. Martin Lake spreads many fingers up the valley of the Tallapoosa, and Lake Harding juts into some parts of Alabama along the Chattahoochee Valley.

Alabama can boast some mountainous country in the northeast. Interesting spurs of the Appalachian range reach into the state. The immense plateau of Lookout Mountain ends in Alabama after crossing three states. Higher regions of northeast Alabama also include parts of the Cumberland Plateau and extensions of the Blue Ridge Mountains.

Cheaha Mountain, 2,407 feet (733.65 meters), near Talladega, is the highest point in the state.

Alabama is divided into four major soil areas—Limestone Valleys and Uplands, Appalachian Plateau, Piedmont Plateau, and Coastal Plains. The Black Belt, a part of the upper Coastal Plain, is known for its dark-colored soils. It was almost the only prairie region of the state when Europeans first found it.

ALABAMA'S FACE IN ANCIENT TIMES

Experts in geology divide Alabama into two geologic provinces—the Coastal Plain and the Appalachian Province. They are separated by a sharp drop known as the fall line which enters Alabama near Phenix City, passes near Wetumpka and Tuscaloosa, and swings into northwest Alabama.

Alabama was once part of the ocean bed. Through the ages some of the northern regions began to rise, and the first dry land in Alabama rose above the water in Precambrian times.

Over the years mountain ranges rose and fell. Ancient seas rolled in and receded. With each rising and falling, more land appeared. Enormous forests grew during the eons. As the forests and large ferns died and fell, layer upon layer of plant matter built up to form peat. As the peat was covered with water, sand, and gravel, the weight of these materials plus chemical action changed the peat to coal.

At last the ancient seas vanished; the rivers flowed, washing away the highlands and building up the coastal plain, the last land in Alabama to be formed. The deltas of the Mobile and Tensaw rivers are current examples of this slow building action.

Although the great glaciers never reached present-day Alabama, they had a noticeable affect upon the land. When they melted, vast quantities of runoff water deposited tremendous amounts of sand, loam, and clay over much of the state.

The glaciers drove many animals south. Hairy mastodons tramped over ridges and made trails which later were followed by buffalo and

Little River Canyon

even Indians. Mastodon fossil skeletons have been found along with such other fossils as the zeuglodon, an enormous whalelike creature.

CLIMATE

There is a wide variation of climate from the highlands of the north to the coastal plain of the Gulf of Mexico. The average number of days between frosts varies from more than three hundred in southern Alabama to about two hundred at the northern boundary. In the southern half the temperature rarely goes below thirty degrees Fahrenheit (minus 1.1 degree Celsius) and snow is so rare that many children have never seen a snow flurry.

In northern Alabama the winters are less mild, but occasional cold snaps are short-lived and usually are followed by mild weather. Infrequent snows do not linger on the ground but soon melt under the Alabama sun.

An Alabama summer is long, but it does not generally have extremes of heat. The warm days are tempered by frequent breezes; even in midsummer, nights are comfortable. Spring comes early and autumn lingers long.

Footsteps on the Land

ANCIENT DWELLERS ON THE LAND

The small man ran in frantic fear; what enemies pursued him we will never know. Suddenly a sharp object pierced his back, bringing unbearable pain. He may have managed to stagger away from his enemies and crawl away to die in his cave home, or friends may have found him and carried his body there.

Refuse and dirt sifted over his body for more than three thousand years until in 1957 scientists from the National Geographic Society uncovered his body in the cavern now known as Russell Cave, a national monument in northeast Alabama. Near his spine still rested the neatly chipped gleaming white stone spear point that had caused his death.

This skeleton, telling its story of an early tragedy, was only one of the many relics of ancient days unearthed in Russell Cave. Here the Geographic scientists have found the earliest remains of life ever discovered in Alabama—reaching back at least ten thousand years.

The record of the lives of peoples who had lived in Russell Cave unfolded from later generations to earlier ones as the scientists dug down from one layer to the next. Some of the objects discovered were similar to items found only in the far north.

Among the most interesting objects of Russell Cave was a bone lamp, fashioned from a part of the hollowed foreleg bone of a bear. Bear fat was packed into the hollow and ignited to form a light for the cave.

The state is dotted with many other sites where prehistoric relics have been found. Places that once were homes of other cave dwellers have been found along many of the bluffs of northern Alabama. These bluff dwellers probably lived about the same time as the shell mound people, who got their name because they ate so many mussels that the discarded shells piled high into mounds. These groups lived two thousand to three thousand years ago. They had little or no agriculture and lived mostly by hunting.

The bluff dwellers were followed by woodland dwellers. On a typical day for the woodland people, the men would leave for their hunt

Russell Cave National Monument

in the forest soon after dawn. They carried bows and arrows, stonetipped spears, and axes of stone. During the day they might bag a raccoon, rabbit, wild turkey, or even a bear or deer. They might have had to settle for a turtle or even a snake. When game was scarce they looked for berries and nuts. They began to cultivate crops in a crude way.

While the men hunted, the women and girls would sift clay through coarse baskets, moisten it, and roll it into ropes. They coiled these in spirals to form jars and other forms of pottery. Then the coils were smoothed. Crude cloth or baskets were pressed into the moist clay to make a pattern and often a design would be scratched onto it. Much of the pottery was painted with red earth.

The women also wove sleeping mats of rushes or cane fiber. With bone needles they sewed deer and other hides into useful objects.

People of several periods in the time just before European exploration belonged to groups known as the Mississippi cultures. These nearly civilized groups raised the many mounds that still dot the Alabama landscape.

Mound State Monument at Moundville preserves one of the finest mound groups in the South. Of the 34 mounds in this group the largest is almost 60 feet (18.28 meters) high and covers an acre and a quarter (.5 hectares) at the base. Engineers estimate that if a hundred men worked ten hours a day it would have taken ten years to build this gigantic mound of earth. It probably supported a ceremonial building or temple.

Another great flat-topped mound, largest on the Tennessee River, is found at Florence.

One of the most interesting prehistoric finds was made in a burial site at Guntersville. Here were buried cowrie shells that were used for money in parts of Africa and Asia. How these seashells could have been brought from their far-off home to a prehistoric Alabama grave has never been explained.

THE CIVILIZED TRIBES

In historic times the region we know as Alabama was inhabited by some of the most advanced Indians of North America. Later they came to be known as the "civilized tribes" because they quickly took on the white man's ways.

The Choctaw laid claim to much of what is now the southern part of the state, even though most of their villages were grouped west of the Tombigbee River. To the north of them lived the Chickasaw, ranked among the great warrior tribes of the world.

The first white men to come into the region brought death and disease to the Indians, and great numbers died. Hearing of this, tribes of Muscogee and Alibamu Indians migrated from Ohio to repeople the abundant forests. They made alliances with the weaker tribes they found in Alabama. These united tribes later were known as the Creek Confederacy. They lived in the central and southeastern part of what is now Alabama and were divided into two major groups, the Upper and Lower Creek.

The Cherokee Indians were also latecomers. Of Iroquois stock, they filtered down into the highland areas of the northeastern part of the state as they were driven from their lands farther to the north and east by the increase of European settlement. William Bartram called them "grave and steady; dignified and circumspect . . . honest, just, and liberal." They had been farming before the Europeans came, and they continued to improve their methods.

The Indians, of a hunting-fishing-farming culture, kept their storehouses full of furs, skins, and feathers and their grain baskets well supplied with food. Some of their chiefs lived in grandeur, draping themselves with strings of freshwater pearls from the Alabama rivers, holding court from chairs placed on raised platforms, and riding from place to place in ornate sedan chairs that were carried by the braves.

Living habits of most of the Alabama tribes were similar. Their houses were of logs. Often their villages were surrounded by fortresslike walls, and the houses faced a ceremonial place or square.

Important among the buildings was the sweat lodge, where the ill were given steam baths, which the Indian thought would cure them; others took the baths to increase their powers.

Most of the tribes raised crops, and the Alabama Indians probably ranked high among the farming peoples of North America. One of their most interesting and novel farm activities was keeping and raising wild turkeys. Early writers reported that some of the flocks numbered in the thousands. Most of them were raised from poults, as young turkeys are called.

A diorama at Mound State Park shows prehistoric life.

Women took charge of gardening, cooking, preparing skins and sewing, gathering firewood, and making baskets and pottery. Men made the hunting and war equipment, fashioned their own smoking pipes, did the construction work, dug out the hollowed trunk pirogues, hunted, traded, and made war. All who were able, both men and women, took part in the planting of the large fields owned by the whole community.

20

BEGINNINGS, LONG DELAYED

As early as 1505 the crude outlines of Mobile Bay were shown on European maps. In 1528 Panfilo de Narvaez led an expedition to the gulf coast, but most of the large group perished. Only four men managed to return to Spanish Mexico.

Hernando de Soto's visit in 1540 left the Indians with hatred for the Spanish people. This may have been one of the reasons for the failure of Tristán de Luna, who in 1559 brought more than one thousand settlers from Mexico and took over the Indian village known as Nanipacana. They did not find the gold they wanted and quarreled constantly among themselves. After three years the settlers gave up and returned to Mexico.

In 1629 the king of England granted to Sir Robert Heath much of the land in this region that had been claimed by Spain, including what was later known as Alabama. Little was done to establish Heath's claim. Ships came in to take on water along the coast, and there probably was considerable trading with the Indians. However, almost 150 years passed between de Luna's settlement and the first real European settlement in Alabama.

Due to the explorations of Robert Cavelier, the Sieur de La Salle, and other French leaders after 1682, France claimed all the region drained by the Mississippi River and west of the Appalachian Mountains.

The French began to establish settlements in the interior all the way from Quebec to the Gulf of Mexico. A fort was set up near what is now Biloxi, Mississippi. Later a settlement was made on Dauphin Island. In 1702 Jean Baptiste Le Moyne, Sieur de Bienville, became governor of the entire French Mississippi Valley empire. He moved his capital from Biloxi to Fort Louis de la Mobile on the Twenty-seven Mile Bluff above the Mobile River.

The Parish of Mobile was organized in 1704. In that same year the little community welcomed one of its most unusual "imports." Because there were no European women in Mobile Parish, the French government encouraged the immigration of French orphan girls by offering each one a *cassette* (small trunk) of clothing if she would go to the New World. Twenty-four Cassette girls landed at Mobile Bay in 1704, and within a month they all were married, with the exception of one who was said to be "coy and hard to please." The others evidently were not too hard to please, since most of the settler-husbands were vagrants, criminals, noblemen who had lost their fortunes, and others of rather doubtful reputation. The first European child born in Alabama was Jean François LeCan. This little native of Fort Louis de la Mobile was born in 1705.

In 1711 Le Moyne moved the capital of Louisiana to the south, setting up Fort Condé de la Mobile where Mobile stands today. The colony did not prosper because most of the settlers spent their time looking for gold or gambling.

In 1712 Louis XIV gave Antoine Crozat, Marquis du Chatel, a charter to develop the Louisiana Territory, including what is now Alabama. He sent Antoine de la Mothe Cadillac, famous founder of Detroit, to be the governor, but Cadillac hated the region and did little to develop it.

However, in 1714 Cadillac set up Fort Toulouse on the Coosa River, in the center of the Creek Confederacy, to protect French interests against the English and the Indians. By this time traders from Mobile were swapping French trade goods with the Indians for their furs, extending this business as far north as Tennessee. Within a few years, as early as 1719, British traders were coming over from Georgia to trade with the Chickasaw. Because the English offered better-quality trade goods to the Indians, the French were constantly in danger of losing their trade. The struggle for the fur trade among the Indians became known as the "Great Fur War."

In 1717 the colony became part of John Law's Mississippi Company, an ambitious scheme to develop the vast area. Within three years the fur trade and plantations growing rice and indigo began to bring French investors a profit, but John Law's complicated schemes in France failed. As a result, France became almost bankrupt.

The colony did not grow enough food to meet its needs; France appeared to forget Louisiana, and the settlers would have starved in 1720 without the generous help of the Choctaw Indians, who loaned corn to the colony.

22

PERIOD OF RAPID CHANGE

Within a few years, however, more and more sugar, rice, and indigo were grown; more furs were traded; and many merchants and plantation owners were becoming wealthy. To do their work they had imported the first six hundred slaves in 1719. In that same year a great Indian Congress had been held at Mobile; the chiefs were given many gifts; the price of trade goods was reduced; and the Indians were encouraged to remain loyal to France.

Mobile was severely afflicted by an epidemic and a hurricane in 1733. Even before this, Mobile had lost its status as capital of Louisiana to mushrooming New Orleans.

In 1736 Bienville led an expedition against the Chickasaw Indians. He hoped to curb the growing power of the English and their allies, but he was severely defeated.

Relations between France and England grew worse, and the two nations went to war in what is known in America as the French and Indian War. By 1763 the French had lost control of the North American continent. The British took over all French territories east of the Mississippi River, and British traders came into Alabama in ever increasing numbers.

The French influence remained strong in Mobile, however. In the 1770s botanist William Bartram wrote an interesting description of Mobile: "The city is situated on the easy ascent of a rising bank, extending near half a mile on the level plain above; it has been near a mile in length, though now chiefly in ruins, many houses vacant and mouldering to earth; yet there are a few good buildings inhabited by French gentlemen, English, Scotch, and Irish, and immigrants from the Northern British Colonies . . ."

The American Revolution was not strongly felt in Alabama, but the war did have some effect. The struggle between the English and the Americans made the Indians restless, and numbers of Americans who were loyal to the British (called Tories) came over into Alabama from Georgia to escape the Revolution. Then in 1780, Governor Galvez of Spanish Louisiana captured Mobile Bay from its British garrison and held it for Spain during the rest of the war.

TECUMSEH.

AN AMERICAN TERRITORY

When the war was over, the 1783 Treaty of Paris recognized that northern Alabama belonged to the new American nation as part of Georgia. However, the British gave Florida to Spain, and so the southern part of Alabama became part of the western territory of Spanish Florida. In 1799 the boundary was surveyed along a line 31° north, and Spain agreed to that location. This boundary was located on what would be an extension of the present northern boundary of the Florida Panhandle, across what is now the Alabama Panhandle.

Congress had formed the Territory of Mississippi in 1798. This included the land between the Florida boundary and 32° 28' north latitude. The territory stretched from the Chattahoochee River on the east to the Mississippi River on the west. President Adams appointed Winthrop Sargent to be the territory's first governor. He was succeeded in 1800 by William C. C. Claiborne.

In 1802 Georgia sold her claims to land west of the Chattahoochee to the Federal government for $1,250,000. In that same year there began another series of treaties in which the United States began to absorb the Choctaw lands.

The land bought from Georgia was added to the Mississippi Territory in 1804, placing the northern boundary of the territory along what is now the Tennessee state line.

When the United States purchased the Louisiana Territory from France in 1803, Federal officials claimed that the Mobile area was included in the purchase; Spain thought otherwise. War with England in 1812 gave the United States an excuse to move in. General James Wilkinson's army captured Mobile in 1813 in a bloodless battle.

THE CREEK WAR

The War of 1812 brought new Indian troubles. West of the Appalachian Mountains the Indians watched with growing horror as white settlers forced them to sign treaties giving up their ancestral lands. The great Shawnee war chief Tecumseh saw the American-British war as an opportunity for the Indians to regain their lands. Even before war broke out he aligned himself with the British and set out to persuade the tribes to unite and drive out the Americans.

In 1811 Tecumseh met with a great tribal council of the Creek at the traditional Creek capital of Tuckabatchee. His British allies had told him just when a comet would appear. When he predicted this, and it came true, he was listened to with some awe. However, the

Tuckabatchee leader, Big Warrior, led the peace group of his nation, and Tecumseh could not get him to agree to go to war.

The angry Tecumseh shouted, "When I get back to Detroit I will stamp my foot upon the ground and shake down every house in Tuckabatchee." By a strange coincidence the worst series of earthquakes in southeastern United States history began in December, 1811, a month after Tecumseh left Tuckabatchee. As the land shook under them it is said that the Indians at Tuckabatchee hurried out of their lodges exclaiming, "Tecumseh has reached Detroit. Feel the earth move with his foot!"

Some branches of the Creek listened to Tecumseh, but other tribes did not. Choctaw Chief Pushmataha denied Tecumseh's plea and, in fact, came to the aid of the Americans. He was greatly influenced by John McKee, United States Indian agent, who also was able to persuade the Chickasaw to side with the Americans.

On July 27, 1813, Americans led by Colonel James Caller attacked a group of Creek at the bend of Burnt Corn Creek near present-day Belleville. They won the first skirmish, but the Indians counterattacked and scattered the Americans.

The Indians, scornful of such a weak people, redoubled their preparations for war. Slaves at Fort Mims, near what is now Bay Minette, who reported that Indians had been seen near the fort on the morning of August 30, 1813, were whipped for lying. The commandant of the fort, a Major Beasley, had heard many reports that the Indians were preparing to attack, but he held the Indians in contempt and did nothing about the rumors.

At noon that day the Indians, led by High Head Jim, Peter MacQueen, and Bill Weatherford, swept into the fort, massacred most of the people there, including Beasley, and took the rest prisoner. They were particularly cruel because many in the fort were part Indian, and considered traitors to their people. The exact death toll in the fort is not known, but some sources place it as high as 553 men, women, and children.

Not long after this the Creek attacked Leslie's Station near present-day Talladega, besieging 14 whites and 125 friendly Indians for many days. Legend tells that one of the Indians, disguised in a pig's

*The last hope of the Creek Nation, this wall fell to the 39th
Regular Infantry Regiment and Tennessee Militia, who in the
Battle of Horseshoe Bend on March 27, 1814, fought hand to hand
to the Tallapoosa River beyond. This final battle of the Creek
Indian War ended the power of the great Creek Confederacy.*

skin, crawled out of the station, grunting and snorting like a pig, and
escaped to notify Andrew Jackson of the station's plight.

Jackson had been assembling volunteers in Tennessee; he
marched at once to help the people of Leslie's Station. Their slogan
was ''Remember Fort Mims.'' In the Battle of Talladega on November 9, 1813, Jackson won the first great success of the Creek War.

The Americans marched farther south, winning other battles as
they went. Finally Jackson and his men met the Indians in the Battle
of Horseshoe Bend, fought on March 27, 1814, near present-day
Dadeville. Both Davy Crockett and Sam Houston took part in this
battle, and Houston was wounded. The Indians were so decisively

beaten in this battle that the power of the great Creek Confederacy was ended. The battle also brought nationwide fame to Andrew Jackson.

Jackson dictated the terms of the Treaty of Fort Jackson, which the Creek were forced to sign on August 9, 1814. The treaty permitted the Creek to keep only a small part of eastern Alabama.

FROM TERRITORY TO STATE

By 1816 the Chickasaw, Cherokee, and Choctaw had given up most of their land in Alabama, and more than three-fourths of the state was opened to settlement.

A Territory of Alabama was organized by Congress on March 3, 1817. President James Monroe selected William Wyatt Bibb to be the first governor of the new territory. The territorial legislature held its first session in 1818 at St. Stephens.

In that same year several pioneers of northern Alabama began to take iron from the ore-bearing red rocks of the region. They built the first smelters near Russellville—forerunners of the giant iron and steel industry in Alabama today.

Only two years after the the territory was established, the population had increased to the point where Congress authorized a state convention at Huntsville to write a constitution for a proposed new state. Congress approved the constitution written by the convention, and on December 14, 1819, President Monroe signed the bill which made Alabama the twenty-second state. Territorial Governor William Bibb became the first elected governor, and the first United States Senators were William Rufus King and John W. Walker.

The official seal of the new state carried a map of Alabama, and today Alabama is the only state to show its own map in the state seal.

Huntsville served as the capital until 1820, when the governmental seat was changed to Cahaba. The United States census in that year recorded the Alabama population as 127,901. In addition to Cahaba, the main communities then were Mobile, Montgomery, Florence, Huntsville, St. Stephens, and Claiborne.

28

Yesterday and Today

PROBLEMS AND OPPORTUNITIES

An event with promise of great things to come was the chugging of the first steamboat up the Alabama River in 1821. With the steamboat the growing number of planters saw that their goods could be moved out more quickly and cheaply than ever before. Also the supplies they needed for building large plantation houses and farming could be moved in with much less time and expense.

Land companies promoted the sale of land, and large numbers of people flocked to the new state of Alabama, many of them people of education and wealth. When America's Revolutionary War hero, the French Marquis de Lafayette, visited Alabama in 1825 he was surprised that already many families were able to live in a luxurious and leisurely manner in new and beautiful homes served by many slaves.

The state of Alabama spent $27,000 to entertain General Lafayette lavishly. A three-hundred-man guard of honor escorted him into Montgomery. Among the crowds lined up to view the great man were many Indians who had been displaced from their homes. Lafayette's secretary said they were very pitiable creatures. The line of march led up Goat Hill, now occupied by the capitol. Americans of the present day would have felt right at home because the band heralded the distinguished guest with *Hail to the Chief!*—now played exclusively for the President.

Governor Israel Pickens greeted Lafayette on the site of the present capitol, but he was so overcome by the thought of the guest's high position that he could not find the voice to make his carefully prepared speech. The honored guest stayed at the fine home of John Edmundson, and a grand ball at Freney's Tavern closed the festivities.

In 1825 Cahaba was seriously damaged by a great flood, and part of the capitol building crumbled. The next year the capital was moved to Tuscaloosa. It was not moved to Montgomery until 1847.

Throughout the southeastern part of the country the period of the 1830s saw one of the saddest chapters in American history—the final removal of the Indians to territory in Oklahoma. Their population at one time was the largest in all of the United States.

In 1830 the Choctaw finally gave up and signed the treaty of Dancing Rabbit Creek. In 1831 the entire tribe gathered near Livingston for three days of wailing and lamentation before they left their ancestral lands for the forbidding dry country of the West.

The Chickasaw also gave up their lands and moved west, keeping their reputation of never having lifted a hand against the English or Americans.

The Creek were forced in 1832 to sign a treaty giving up their lands. Eager settlers from Georgia broke the terms of the treaty by moving in too soon and there were a number of skirmishes with the Indians. To the south the Seminole Indians in revolt were led by an Alabama native, the famous Osceola. A number of Creek people went south to join the Seminole in the bitter Seminole War. For a time it looked as if the Seminole War might spread northward into Alabama. However, Governor Clay and General Winfield Scott persuaded the Creek Indians to keep the peace, and eventually they were moved as they had agreed earlier.

While they were being moved in 1836, one group of several hundred Creek was attacked without cause or warning by a company of local militia. They fought bravely but most of them were killed. Some were allowed to go on to Oklahoma, but others were held in prison, and one was found in a state of slavery as late as 1873.

The majority of the Cherokee refused to sign a treaty, but a small group of them was persuaded to sign, and the government used this as an excuse to round them all up in concentration camps. They were then sent off to the West in the "Great Removal."

These Indian tribes who lived in Alabama, especially the Cherokee, were among the most civilized of all American Indians. Many in each of the civilized tribes lived in fine plantation houses, cultivated as many as ten thousand acres (4,047 hectares), and even owned slaves. They had their own constitutions, laws and courts, and built substantial towns. In many cases greedy settlers without any authorization took over Indian homes and plantations while the Indian owners were still there.

30

But soon the Indians were out of sight and out of mind, and their many improvements had passed on to other "owners."

PROCEEDING TOWARD CONFLICT

Another racial problem faced the nation ever more menacingly as time went on. Alabama was a slave state, but it was a state of small slave holders. Only 34 planters owned more than 200 slaves. Most owned only four or five. A total of 435,000 slaves almost equaled Alabama's white population of only 526,431. There were only 2,690 free black people in all of Alabama.

In northern Alabama many people believed in the freeing of slaves. Many such Alabamians belonged to the Alabama Colonization Society, a state branch of the American Colonization Society, devoted to colonizing former slaves. The Tuscaloosa Monitor declared: "We believe that the Southern States themselves would be better off without this institution (slavery) than with it. We feel confident that, if it had no present existence with us, a large majority of the Southern people would be found opposed to its introduction."

Probably the strongest opposition to slavery in Alabama came from the hill and mountain people of the northeast. Even when war came, many of them avoided the Confederate Army draft.

However, when relations between North and South reached the breaking point, Alabama was ready. Delegates were elected who met in convention on January 7, 1861. On January 11, the convention voted to secede from the Union, and Alabama became the fourth state to take this step. Its Senators and Representatives in Washington resigned, and for a few weeks Alabama was an independent republic, flying its own flag, until soon after it joined the Confederacy.

On February 4, delegates of six of the seceded states met at Montogomery and selected that city to be the first capital of the Confederate States of America. On February 9, delegates chose Jefferson Davis as President of the Confederacy.

Montgomery was wild with excitement when Jefferson Davis arrived. He was escorted with a torchlight parade and famed orator

William L. Yancey proclaimed, "The man and the hour have met!" At 1:00 P.M. on February 16, he stood on the porch of the capitol, where now a brass star marks the spot, and took his oath of office as President.

An Alabama resident, Nichola Marschall of Marion, designed a Confederate flag, suggested by Mrs. Napoleon Lockett of Marion. The stars and bars were sewn together hastily and raised for the first time in triumph over the capitol on March 4, 1861.

Alabama had become the "cradle of the Confederacy."

ALABAMA AT WAR

From a building on Market Street near the artesian basin in the Confederate capital, a telegram went out that authorized the firing on Fort Sumter in Charleston, South Carolina. The severed nation was at war.

Alabama state troops captured Forts Morgan and Gaines which guarded the entrance to Mobile Bay. Regiments were formed and drilled; supplies were assembled; the production of iron and other wartime goods was stepped up. The state began every possible preparation for war.

War did not come immediately within Alabama's boundaries, but Alabama's men joined all the major forces of the Confederacy. Possibly as many as 125,000 men from Alabama fought in Confederate service. The number of dead is placed as high as 70,000. Surprisingly, 2,500 white and 10,000 black soldiers from Alabama served with the Union forces.

Union Colonel A. D. Streight made a raid in northeast Alabama in 1863. He sacked Gadsden and left the city on the eastern boundary just as Confederate General Nathan Bedford Forrest entered the city from the other side.

When Streight appeared to be heading for Rome, Georgia, Confederate mail contractor John H. Wisdom jumped on his horse and made a ride which is as famous in the South as that of Paul Revere. Through the night Wisdom galloped over 67 miles (about 108

The Battle of Mobile Bay

kilometers) of rocky and unfamiliar roads. He left Gadsden at 3:30 P. M. and arrived in Rome at midnight. Rome heard his warning and prepared for attack.

A confederate heroine of the Gadsden conflict was Emma Sansom. Streight had burned the Black Creek Bridge, and fifteen-year-old Emma volunteered to lead the Confederate soldiers to a ford across the creek. Almost struck by a bullet, she shouted, "They've only wounded my dress!" Then she waved her sunbonnet at the Union men. Both sides cheered and stopped firing until she was out of the way.

Streight found Rome warned and ready; he turned back to face Forrest, who had only about three hundred men compared to the Union's fourteen hundred. Forrest marched various groups of his men so that it would appear he had a large force. Streight and his men, who were completely exhausted, surrendered.

In 1864 General Forrest used a similar trick to fool a force under Union Colonel Campbell near Athens. Forrest had his men pass by as cavalry; then he had them dismount and appear as infantry. Campbell thought he was hopelessly outnumbered and surrendered.

On August 5, 1864, Union Admiral David Farragut moved his thirteen wooden ships and four ironclads into the entrance of Mobile Bay. The Union flagship Hartford was raked by fire from the guardian forts, Morgan and Gaines, by the Confederate ironclad Tennessee, and three small gunboats in the harbor. The Confederates were commanded by Admiral Franklin Buchanan. This was one of the last battles in which wooden warships proved successful, but even here the ironclad played a more important role than the other ships. In spite of the Confederate fire, by 10:00 A. M. the entrance to the port had fallen to Union forces. For his victory at Mobile Bay David Glasgow Farragut became the first full admiral of the American Navy. The city of Mobile did not fall until it was captured by Union Generals E. R. S. Canby and F. Steele on April 12, 1865. Generals Canby and Steele were victorious over Confederate General D. H. Maury.

On that same day Union General James Wilson's raiders entered Montgomery. Selma had fallen two days earlier. The iron-covered warship that fought Farragut in Mobile Bay had been built in Selma. General John H. Croxton captured Tuscaloosa on April 4 and burned all except four of the state university buildings. He said this order had come from higher authority. The wife of the university president, Mrs. Landon C. Garland, persuaded the Federal troops to save the president's house; she pointed out that their orders called for them to burn only public buildings.

After General Robert E. Lee's surrender in Virginia, the war moved rapidly toward a close.

AWFUL AFTERMATH

Alabama had suffered a fearful toll of war dead, money spent, and property destroyed. The old plantation system of agriculture was useless without slaves, and business was at a standstill. The newly freed slaves were suddenly responsible for themselves, and most of them lacked experience in caring for their own needs. A single shack might be the home of many families who did not have even the bare necessities of life.

When Alabama refused to approve the 14th Amendment to the United States Constitution, the Federal government placed the state under military rule. Unscrupulous people from the North, known as carpetbaggers because they carried all their possessions in a carpetbag, swarmed in to take advantage of both white and black. Many local people, called scalawags, also took advantage of the situation for their own benefit.

The 14th Amendment was approved. The carpetbag administration of Governor William Hugh Smith misused public funds and encouraged black people to resent white people and to organize into societies. White people organized groups such as the Ku Klux Klan and the Knights of the White Camellia to offset black influence. Racial tensions grew and have not yet been entirely eased.

Federal troops were not withdrawn from Alabama until 1876. By this time there had been a slow but steady recovery from the war and the effects of the Reconstruction period.

A MODERN STATE

Birmingham had been founded in 1871, beginning a new era of industry in the South. The state quickly adapted to modern ways, as shown by such examples as Montgomery's trolley system installed in 1886—the first electric streetcar system in the world.

The first steel from Alabama was produced at North Birmingham in 1888. The iron and steel city of Bessemer had been started just the year before.

The first iron was exported from Alabama in 1896, and in that same year the first hydroelectric power was generated.

When President William McKinley called for army volunteers to fight in the war with Spain, the hatred from the Civil War had diminished considerably and Alabama responded with two regiments of volunteers. One batallion was made up of black volunteers.

The people ratified a new state constitution in 1901, and on the 200th anniversary of the founding of Fort Louis de la Mobile, Mobile celebrated.

The long established cotton industry was shaken when the boll weevil was brought in from Mexico in 1910. Cotton growing declined and other crops became more important.

In 1916 Congress authorized the use of twenty million dollars to build Wilson Dam at Muscle Shoals and to create a hydroelectric plant whose power could be used for manufacturing nitrates. The nitrate would have been useful in World War I, which America entered a year later, but the plant was not finished by the war's end. Nevertheless, manufacture of nitrates and electric power there later assumed great importance.

The first member of the United States Navy to give his life in World War I was an Alabama man—Seaman Osmond Kelly (O. K.) Ingram. Altogether, 86,916 Alabamians saw military service during the war, and many lost their lives.

In the years after the war there was considerable progress: a new Child Welfare Department, establishment of workmen's compensation, creation of the modern port of Mobile, and the abolishment of the convict leasing system.

36

The state witnessed several disasters which included the great floods of 1929 and several hurricanes and tornadoes. The tornado of 1932 killed 315 people and injured 3,000.

In 1933 the Tennessee Valley Authority, known as TVA, was established. Its purpose was to help overcome the effects of the Great Depression of the early 1930s. The key to this whole project was the work already done at Wilson Dam. Throughout the valley other great dams were built, along with power plants and locks and channels for navigation.

During this period a number of events forecast a change in relations between the races. In the famous Scottsboro case, decided by the United States Supreme Court in 1932, the judgment of the Alabama Supreme Court was reversed and nine black men were returned for a new trial because the Federal court said their original trial was unfair and prejudiced. Four were released, and five were convicted.

In the years of World War II Alabama sent 288,003 into United States service, and many of these gave their lives.

On January 31, 1958, Alabama played an important role in launching the United States into the Space Age. On that date Explorer I, the West's first satellite, was launched into orbit by a modified Jupiter missile. The satellite and the rocket had been developed at Huntsville at the Army Ballistic Missile Agency under the direction of rocket expert Dr. Wernher von Braun.

Crowds thronged the streets of the once sleepy cotton town of Huntsville in an emotional celebration. Sirens screamed and fireworks were set off. The United States was in the space race and Huntsville was leading the way.

A celebration of another kind was held in Birmingham in 1961. This was America's first statewide Festival of Sacred Music.

In 1965 Governor George Wallace conducted a campaign to save the famous World War II battleship bearing the state's name. The U. S. S. *Alabama* was scheduled to be scrapped by the navy. However, with the help of pennies and dimes from 500,000 Alabama school children, the ship was saved and brought into Mobile Bay as a memorial to the war dead and a symbol of the state.

Lights outline the battleship U. S. S. Alabama *in Mobile Bay.*

The year 1967 saw one of the most striking events in the recent political history of Alabama, whose state politics have received considerable national attention. On January 16, 1967, Lurlcen B. Wallace took the oath of office as Alabama's forty-eighth governor. Her husband, George Wallace, had preceded her as governor. He was not permitted by the state constitution to serve another term. He ran for President in 1968, and began another long term as governor in 1971, permitted by a change in the state constitution.

Development of the Saturn engine in Alabama led directly to the first moon landing on July 20, 1969. The Marshall Space Flight Center continued, on a somewhat lesser scale, with the development of the space shuttle the major project of the late 1970s.

THE PEOPLE OF ALABAMA

Very few people in Alabama were born outside the United States. The state has one of the highest percentages of native-born residents.

Most of the white population are descendants of the people of northern Europe, especially the British Isles. The people of German and Canadian descent are fairly numerous. Others include a scattering of peoples of Italian, Greek, Polish, Austrian, and French ancestry.

More than a quarter of Alabama's people are black.

Relatively few communities of ethnic groups were established in Alabama. One of the most interesting of these was Demopolis (City of the People), founded by the Association of French Emigrants for the Cultivation of the Vine and Olive. A large group of these exiled supporters of Napoleon Bonaparte arrived at Mobile in the ship *McDonough* in 1817. They made their way into the wilderness. Not one of these aristocratic people had ever worked with his hands. Only the help of their "rustic" neighbors and the kindness of the Choctaw Indians kept them from disaster. They had difficulty in proving title to their land and finally they had to give up.

The city of Cullman was named for John Cullman, who was instrumental in bringing large numbers of German people to the Cullman region. The county was also named in his honor.

One of the most interesting groups in Alabama are the Cajuns. These are not related to the Cajuns of Louisiana who came from Acadia. The Alabama Cajuns are probably descended from early Spanish, French, and English settlers who married Indian women. They have had a difficult time supporting themselves, mostly in lumbering and producing turpentine. They keep much to themselves.

Of the great Indian population which once thronged Alabama, only about twenty-four hundred remain. Creek Indians keep to themselves and have their own "chief."

The main national civil rights organizations have found supporters in Alabama for their varied programs. At the present time, school systems in Alabama include black students and faculty. Yet predominantly black schools and colleges continue to serve large proportions of black communities.

An Alabama black community of poignant and unusual history is Africky Town. Many residents of the community trace their ancestry to the last shipload of slaves brought into the South on Captain Tim Meaher's ship *Clotilde*. Bringing in new slaves had been illegal since 1807, but the abominable business continued. Captain Meaher burned the *Clotilde* and hid the slaves, but could not find buyers for most of them. Left to make their own way, they developed Africky Town.

Cudjo Lewis, who died in 1935 at the age of one hundred and five, was the last of the original settlers of the town. A devoted churchman, he knew many chapters of the Bible by heart.

Natural Treasures

LIVING THINGS

Among Alabama's many distinctions are two minor but interesting rare plants. The *neviusia Alabamensis* is found only in Alabama. This deciduous shrub is so rare that it does not even have a common name. An evergreen shrub known as *croton Alabamensis* also knows no other home but Alabama.

In the spring the blooming shrubs and trees make the state almost a continual garden. During February and March the spectacular Mobile Azalea Trail draws many tourists.

Rhodendron bearing great clusters of flowers grow to tree height in the highlands. Mountain laurel adds its pink bloom to the blossoming season. Although the azalea is not native to Alabama, probably no other region is so noted for its displays of this highly cultivated and spectacularly blooming plant. Not so admired is the appropriately named stinking laurel.

In spite of generations of cutting and much waste in earlier days, twenty-two million acres (nearly nine million hectares) of forests still flourish in Alabama. Some of the finest areas are protected in the four national forests—Talladega, William B. Bankhead, Conecuh, and Tuskegee.

Major trees of Alabama include longleaf-slash pine, loblolly-shortleaf pine, oak-pine, oak-hickory, and oak-gum-cypress. A few virgin forests of longleaf pine remain. These resemble beautiful, cultivated parks, where the trees grow strong and straight several feet (a few meters) apart, as if planted by men. There is almost no underbrush.

Much admired in Alabama are the magnificent magnolia grandiflora with its huge waxy blossoms, and the extremely rare yellow-blooming magnolia. Altogether, Alabama has more native trees than all of Europe, and most of them can still be found growing wild in the forests.

Wildflowers of the state are profuse, and there are 275 varieties of ferns, liverworts, and mosses, along with 1,500 kinds of lichens and fungi. The natural abundance of flowers has promoted the development of gardens, such as famed Bellingrath Gardens in Mobile County.

The best-known Alabama songbirds are mockingbirds and thrashers. Most of the birds common to the South and Midwest are abundant, as well as the wading birds and shore birds found along the gulf coast. Mobile Bay and the islands of the shore shelter these by the thousands. Many types of northern birds never come farther south than the Warrior tableland.

Ducks, geese, quail, and wild turkey are found in numbers that delight the hunters. Deer is the principal game animal. A highly efficient conservation organization uses boats, autos, airplanes, and radios to protect and increase the state's game and fish.

Excellent fishing is found in the 24,000 miles (about 38,624 kilometers) of Alabama rivers and creeks. The huge man-made lakes are well stocked with fish, where world-record smallmouth bass, largemouth bass, crappie, and other native gamefish are abundant. Near the dams, monster catfish are found.

A swan adds to the beauty of Bellingrath Gardens in Mobile County.

Speckled trout thrive in the brackish tidal waters of southern Alabama. In the deep-sea waters of the gulf kingfish tarpon, bonita, and other fish can be caught.

In the commercial field, the Bon Secour oysters of the Mobile area have been called the best oysters in America.

The king of the reptiles, the alligator, is becoming more and more rare, as are the mammoth sea turtles that come to the shore to lay their eggs. Many harmless and helpful snakes are found, but there are three of the more deadly varieties—rattlers, coral snakes, and moccasins.

MINERAL WEALTH

The Indians used to use the red rocks of Alabama for paint. These red rocks later proved to be iron ore—one of the state's greatest treasures. The iron ore reserves of Alabama are still extensive. Although the red ore, known as hematite, is the most abundant in Alabama, there are also supplies of brown ore, limonite, and gray ore. Some of the state's iron ore can be observed even within the city limits of Birmingham, where open cuts have been made into iron-bearing hills.

Coal fields, the other "Big Twin" mineral, begin in about the middle of the state and extend to the Tennessee Valley. If all of Alabama's coal reserves could be dug up and spread out, they would cover the whole of England to a depth of three feet (nearly one meter). In addition, there are an estimated 200 million short tons (about 182 million metric tons) of low-grade coal known as lignite which may someday be widely used.

The very important limestone, as well as dolomite, marble, glass sand, graphite, kaolin, kyanite, ocher, fuller's earth, fluorite, corundum, greensand, bauxite, lead, and even small quantities of gold and tin are found. There are a few small petroleum bearing areas.

One of the most valuable of all Alabama's minerals is a superabundance of high quality fresh water, both for household use and for industry's ever-growing water needs.

42

People Use Their Treasures

IN VULCAN'S REALM

It is no accident that Vulcan, god of the forge, raises his hammer over Birmingham in a mighty statue, for Alabama offers work to many thousands of Vulcans. It is the only state blessed in one area with all the materials man needs to make iron and steel.

Iron ore, coal, and limestone are abundant in the Birmingham region, but they are found together in sufficient quantities nowhere else in the country.

It probably could be said that the iron "industry" in the state started when the first Indian painted his face with the red iron rocks. But Alabama's first real iron furnace was not begun until 1818 near Russellville. By the time of the Civil War, sixteen ironworks were busy with armament, and the ironworks of Alabama performed the vital task of providing most of the iron available to the Confederacy.

Small quantities of steel were produced in Alabama as early as 1888, and large-scale steel mills using the Bessemer process began operation in 1899. Today Alabama produces almost 4,000,000 short tons (3,628,800 metric tons) of steel each year, and Birmingham is known as the Pittsburgh of the South. Other leading iron and steel centers are Bessemer, Anniston, and Gadsden.

The tremendous quantity of cast-iron pipe turned out in the Anniston area and elsewhere in the state makes Albama first in the production of this material.

Total value of all manufacturing in Alabama in the latest available figures reached $5,063,900,000. Primary metals, including iron and steel, accounted for $806,100,000 of this; next were coal and petroleum at $264,400,000; followed by textiles, $457,400,000; food industry, $368,800,000; and pulp and paper, $468,800,000. One of the world's largest pulp and paper mills operates at Mobile.

Other important industries include apparel, rubber, lumber, fabricated metals, transportation equipment, stone, clay and glass, non-electrical machinery, and printing and publishing.

Alabama is making continuing gains in manufacturing. Over the last several years an average of two new industrial plants have

Statue of Vulcan in Birmingham

opened in Alabama every week. Gadsden, Birmingham, and Tuscaloosa, with their suburbs, form an industrial belt that extends almost entirely across the state, as does the Tennessee Valley to the north.

The textile industry appeared in Alabama in 1809, ten years before statehood, with a tiny cotton mill built along the Flint River in Madison County. The first large plant was built in 1850 at Autaugaville. It could handle 1,200 bales of cotton a year. Just before the Civil War, Alabama's cotton mills had a total of 35,700 spindles whirring in fourteen different plants.

One of Alabama's more unusual industries is the world's largest ground-oyster-shell plant at Mobile.

A bright spot in Alabama's industrial picture is the coal industry, which has staged a comeback and is producing 21,425,479 tons (19,437,194 metric tons) a year. At the present rate, surface coal reserves will last two hundred years and underground coal sixteen hundred years.

ROCKET CITY, USA

Only a few hundred years ago on the site where Huntsville stands today people were laboriously chipping away hard stones to form arrows to shoot at game. Now on that same site men have worked just as hard to produce a dramatic new kind of "arrow" designed to shoot at the moon.

What would the prehistoric hunter think if he could come back today? The transformation from bow and arrow to moon rocket scarcely can be understood by those who have followed the project from its beginning.

With these developments the recent history of Huntsville has been most dramatic. A small Alabama city has been transformed into the "Rocket Capital of the Nation—Rocket City, USA."

In 1950, 120 German rocket scientists headed by Dr. Wernher von Braun arrived at the Huntsville Arsenal. Hundreds of American scientists also moved to Huntsville and the big push to produce rockets began. In February, 1956, the Army Ballistic Missile Agency (ABMA) was activated at Redstone. With the West's first successful orbital flight out of the way in 1958, ABMA began work on an immense rocket booster to produce 1,500,000 pounds (680,400 kilograms) of thrust, the first part of a multistage booster to put an American on the moon. This was to be called the Saturn. The National Aeronautics and Space Administration (NASA) took over in 1959, and in 1960 the Huntsville center became known as the George C. Marshall Space Flight Center.

In 1950 Huntsville covered 4 square miles (about 10 square kilometers) and contained 16,437 persons. Today the corporate limits encircle nearly 105 square miles (more than 270 square kilometers) and approximately 146,000 persons live there, with 292,000 in the metropolitan area.

Now the Saturn rocket is history; the space station has diminished its activity, but an increased effort has brought substantial new industry to the area.

AGRICULTURE

Throughout most of its history Alabama has depended on agriculture for most of its income. However, a change from the farm to the city has rapidly taken place in the last few years.

Nevertheless, agriculture remains important. Farm income in Alabama in 1976 was expected to hit a resounding $2 billion. Of this about $700 million was from livestock and more than $.5 billion from crops.

Cotton accounts for more than $100 million of income for the state. It is now the state's second most valuable crop, with soybeans now "king" of Alabama's row crops in cash income, and peanuts third.

Alabama claims to be the third-largest producer of chicken broilers, and 1974 income from broilers was $295,208,000 from 400 million broilers. Eggs brought in another $128,963,000 and cattle and calves $90,000,000.

The Space Museum at Huntsville

For many years the history of agriculture in Alabama was almost entirely the history of cotton. Beginning in 1800 there was a rapid growth of cotton production. Alabama's many river valleys and the lime-rich soils of its famous Black Belt were superbly suited to the growing of cotton; the state's flourishing cotton economy reached its peak in the 1840s and 1850s.

To have an accurate understanding of the significance of cotton, it must be realized that not only was it the principal cash crop for Alabama and all southern states, but also provided tens of thousands of jobs in cotton mills in New England as well as in Great Britain.

Following the Civil War, Alabama's once prosperous cotton economy lay shattered. Plantation owners had no money; the former slave class was free, but without education or jobs. Out of this situation was born the tenant farm system.

Mechanization brought about the demise of the tenant farm system. Today most workers have moved into urban areas and cotton is planted and harvested by gigantic diesel-powered machines.

Cotton may not be king anymore, but it is still a vital part of Alabama's total economy.

TRANSPORTATION AND COMMUNICATION

"Finest river system in the nation," is Alabama's claim for its 1,213 miles (1,952 kilometers) of navigable waterways. The four great river systems of Black Warrior-Tombigbee, Tennessee, Alabama, and Chattahoochee provide channels that are deep enough for commercial barges. Nearly 50 million tons (about 46 million metric tons) of freight move on these waterway systems each year. Even inland Birmingham has a port on the Black Warrior River.

Prehistoric peoples used the waterways, and the earliest Europeans in the region found they were the best avenues of transportation. Flatboats known as keelboats carried a lot of freight in the early days. They were as long as 150 feet (about 46 meters) and were about 10 feet (three meters) wide. On the narrower rivers, men stood in the front of the keelboats, reached out with long poles with

*The Alabama Dry Dock and Shipbuilding Company
builds new oceangoing ships and services world shipping.*

hooks on the end, hooked onto trees or bushes on the bank, and pulled the keelboat upstream. From this practice has come the term "bushwhacking."

Montgomery celebrated the sight of its first steamboat in 1821, and from that time on steamboats were used until they reached their peak in about 1850. Steamers on the Alabama River became increasingly luxurious and faster, setting new speed records on almost every run.

Mobile, Alabama's only seaport, is one of the major ports of the nation, ranking eleventh among the country's ocean ports and handling more than 20 million tons (about 18 million metric tons) of freight a year. Thirty-two ocean vessels can tie up at one time in the spacious port of Mobile.

Alabama's southern heel is transversed by the Gulf Intracoastal Waterway, which brings much freight to port and rivers.

Early land travelers in Alabama followed the trails made by the Indians, who used the buffalo paths. Buffalo seemed to know by instinct the most direct and safest routes. Best known of the Indian roads was the Natchez Trace, running from Nashville, Tennessee, to Natchez, Mississippi. In 1801 the Federal government purchased this road from the Indians, and it was Alabama's only wagon road for more than ten years. Today, the route of the Natchez Trace is followed by a modern national parkway.

Another historic route was the Old Spanish Trail, or the King's Highway, cutting across southern Alabama on a route that took the Spaniards across the continent.

Much later, Montgomery had regular stagecoach service to Nashville and Columbus, Georgia. About every twelve miles (nineteen kilometers) along stagecoach routes there were relay stations to provide changes of horses.

Senator John H. Bankhead, Sr., was a leader in the movement to provide good roads for Alabama. Today the state is crisscrossed by four routes of the great interstate system as well as thousands of miles (thousands of kilometers) of federal and state highways.

The first railroad tracks ever placed west of the Allegheny Mountains were laid in Alabama. These were the tracks of the Tuscumbia Railway, which received its charter in 1830. Forty-four miles (about seventy-one kilometers) of this line had been built from Decatur to Tuscumbia before the close of 1834.

Today, the seventeen railroads operating in Alabama have a total trackage of more than forty-five hundred miles (over seven thousand kilometers)—more than any other southwest state except Georgia.

"Flagport" of the many modern airports of Alabama is busy Birmingham airport, only fifteen minutes from downtown. In the southeast it is fourth in total activity and operations. It has offices of many major airlines.

Settlement had continued in what is now Alabama for over a hundred years before the printing firm of Miller and Hood began to publish the first newspaper of the territory. The initial issue appeared on May 23, 1811, and was produced at Fort Stoddert.

50

Human Treasures

A NEW GRACE IN THE HUMAN SPIRIT

In 1880 a baby girl was born at Tuscumbia who was to become one of the most famous and best-loved women of all time. Mark Twain called her the greatest woman since Joan of Arc. She was famous from the age of ten, when a ship was named for her and Queen Victoria inquired about her. She had sat on the lap of Oliver Wendell Holmes, and he published one of her letters in a book. During her life, eight Presidents received her in the White House. Other rulers and leaders of most of the world paid tribute to her. Books, plays, and motion pictures have dealt with her life.

Yet this great woman, Helen Adams Keller, was six years old before she knew anything at all about the world around her. At the age of eighteen months she had an illness which left her blind and deaf. Since no one could talk to her or make her understand anything, she understood nothing of what was going on. Someone has called her "a small wild animal."

Then her mother heard of a method of teaching the deaf and blind. The story of Anne Sullivan, the teacher who came to Tuscumbia in 1887 to teach little Helen, is almost as well known as Helen Keller's own life. Within a month "the vixen had been transformed into a gentle child." Anne taught Helen that things had names, that there were such things as ideas. She roamed through the woods and fields, feeling the grass, water, animals—even the vibrations in an egg as a newly born chick pecked its way out. She enjoyed the odors of the outdoors.

By a method of tapping out letters and words on her hand, Helen Keller had learned German, Latin, Greek, and French by the time she was ten. The fame of her accomplishments soon spread around the world.

At twelve she gave a tea party that raised $2,000 for the blind. She was introduced to famous people who took great interest in her, and in a group she could recognize everyone by a handshake.

Helen Keller's character was almost as remarkable as her accomplishments. She was said to be physically and morally fearless.

51

Helen Keller's cottage in Tuscumbia

Even at the age of seven she refused to stop until she had mastered what she was doing. She felt that whatever anyone else was able to do she could do also. Far from being subdued by her handicap, she loved to climb trees, run, dive, and swim underwater.

Perhaps, however, her greatest characteristic was her deep interest in other people. Mark Twain wrote that she had brought "a new grace in the human spirit." The accomplishments of the little blind and deaf girl from Alabama who rose to greatness and yet remained humble and interested in helping others will long be an inspiration to all, whether handicapped in some way or not.

BUILDERS OF A CIVILIZATION

In 1881 a young educator arrived at Tuskegee, ready to take over as the head of a college. He found that the school did not yet exist; there was no building, no land; the state legislature was providing only two thousand dollars per year, which had to be used for salaries.

The young man, whose name was Booker Taliaferro as a slave and who had since added the name of Washington, was disappointed but not defeated. He went out immediately to get support for the new school at Tuskegee and found thirty students for the "school that didn't exist." The African Methodist Episcopal Zion Church loaned them a building that Mr. Washington said was "in such disrepair that, when rain fell, one of the older students held an umbrella over the teacher while he listened to the recitation of the others."

Later, Mr. Washington found an old plantation with only a hen house on a hundred acres (about forty hectares) of land. It was on the market for five hundred dollars. The college group bought it, cleaned the hen house, and made it a school.

The black community made many sacrifices to help pay this five hundred dollars. Probably no contribution touched Mr. Washington so much as the gift of six eggs from an elderly woman who had nothing else to give.

Booker T. Washington and his students cleared the land so that crops could be grown to feed the students and faculty. Later they

Booker T. Washington, founder and head of Tuskeegee Institute

made bricks from clay on the land, built a kiln with money from Mr. Washington's pawned watch, and fired millions of bricks to build buildings for Tuskegee Institute.

As the institute grew so did the respect of the whole community for Booker T. Washington. Presidents William McKinley and

Theodore Roosevelt visited Tuskegee Institute to see how young men and women were taught not only practical skills but also were given a knowledge of a wider world which many of them had never before glimpsed.

Booker T. Washington was invited to be the first black man ever to address a mixed general audience in the South, at the opening of the International Cotton Exposition at Atlanta in 1895. The speech he made there brought wide approval.

However, in that speech Washington spoke some words that seem wise and wonderful to many but that many others dislike: ". . . progress in the enjoyment of all the privileges that will come to us must be the result of severe and constant struggle rather than of artificial forcing. No race that has anything to contribute to the markets of the world is long, in any degree, ostracized. It is important and right that all privileges of the law be ours, but it is vastly more important that we be prepared for the exercise of those privileges. The opportunity to earn a dollar in a factory just now is worth infinitely more than the opportunity to spend a dollar in an opera house."

Those who objected to his "severe and constant struggle" and who felt that progress by blacks could be made only by "artificial forcing" never forgave Booker T. Washington for those words. While he is revered by many, he is ridiculed by an impatient few.

Yet fifty years after his death, the educational paths blazed by Booker T. Washington are being tried once more in struggling nations around the world.

One of this wise teacher's gifts was the ability to choose staff members at Tuskegee. One of these was to become a world figure in his own right. On April 1, 1896, Booker T. Washington wrote to young Iowa scientist George Washington Carver: ". . . I offer you. . . work—hard, hard work—the task of bringing a people from degradation, poverty, and waste to full manhood."

So George Washington Carver went to Tuskegee. In his years there, he revolutionized the agriculture of wide areas and gained a reputation as one of the world's great agricultural scientists. He found 300 new uses for peanuts and 175 for sweet potatoes. He turned down large salaries from big corporations, refused increases of his salary at Tuskegee, and continued his work there where he felt he could give the greatest service to his people. He died in 1943, after forty-seven years of service to the institute and to the world at large.

THREE FOR THE CANAL

Alabama men played an unusual part in the building of the Panama Canal.

The French had to give up their efforts to build the canal. One of the causes of their failure was yellow fever. This disease had made it impossible for them to continue the work. When the United States took over the job, the country's leaders realized something must be done about yellow fever or they would succeed no better than the French had.

Dr. Walter Reed had discovered that yellow fever was carried through the bite of Stegomyia mosquito, and Dr. William Crawford Gorgas, during American occupation of Cuba in 1898, had freed Havana from yellow fever by clearing up all the breeding places of the mosquito.

Dr. Gorgas was born at Toulminville, Alabama, in 1854. Serving in the United States Army at Fort Brown, Texas, he had lived through an attack of yellow fever. This gave him an immunity to yellow fever and he was often sent to bases where there were yellow fever epidemics. He became well acquainted with the disease.

In 1904 Dr. Gorgas was asked to help in the Panama Canal Zone. He decided that total destruction of the mosquito population was necessary to prevent the spread of the disease. Strangely, few people believed in his work and he had little help from officials. But he set to work with a small army of helpers, pouring oil on mosquito breeding places, draining swamps, clearing out every possible place mosquitoes could hatch. After this monumental task was over, it was discovered that Dr. Gorgas had made the Canal Zone one of the healthiest places in the tropics.

Noted as one of the world's top sanitation engineers, Dr. Gorgas became Surgeon General of the Army and later helped in important sanitation projects throughout the world.

Without the work in Congress of another Alabama man, United States Senator John T. Morgan, the canal might not have been undertaken in the first place.

General William L. Sibert, native of the Gadsden area, first came to public attention when he supervised the building of the giant Gatun Locks for the Panama Canal. Congress gave him a special vote of thanks for heroic work in World War I. Also during his career he helped in constructing the Great Lakes Ship Canal and was in charge of the commission for building Hoover Dam. One of the great builders of modern times, General Sibert also planned the port of Mobile when he was chief engineer for the Alabama State Docks Commission.

OTHERS IN THE PUBLIC EYE

United States Senator John H. Bankhead married Tallulah Brockman at the Presbyterian church in Wetumpka in 1866. Senator Bankhead was known as the father of the federal road system. U. S. route 78, extending from Washington to San Diego and cutting across Alabama through Birmingham, was named in his honor.

His son John H. Bankhead, Jr., also became a United States Senator. The brother of John, Jr., was William B. Bankhead, who held many high positions in the House of Representatives, including chairman of the rules committee, Majority Leader, and Speaker of the House—1936 to his death in 1940. He came close to receiving the Democratic nomination for Vice President under Franklin Delano Roosevelt in 1940.

Will Bankhead's daughter, born at Jasper near Birmingham in 1903, earned fame in an entirely different field. Tallulah Brockman Bankhead, named for her grandmother, gained worldwide recognition for her brilliant acting in stage plays such as *The Little Foxes* and movie hits such as *Lifeboat.*

In addition to the Bankheads, many prominent Alabama men have served in Congress. In 1940 Senator Lister Hill nominated President Franklin D. Roosevelt for his controversial third term as President. Senator Hugo Lafayette Black became one of the best-known judges of the United States Supreme Court.

An earlier legislator who carried great weight in the United States Senate was Dixon H. Lewis, from near Montgomery. Lewis weighed 500 pounds (about 226 kilograms). His seat in Congress had to be specially made to hold him and his carriage had to have special springs. There was a joke among the legislators that Alabama had the largest representation in Congress of any state.

Another Alabama public figure was William Rufus King, who served as Senator and then as Vice President of the United States. King also founded and named the town of Selma, Alabama.

One of the amusing sidelights of Alabama's political history came when Democratic Senator Morgan was to meet Republican Napoleon (Nap) Mardis in a debate at a great barbecue held at Shelby Springs. Morgan began to speak in the morning and kept on until the crowd could hardly bear the delicious aroma of barbecuing beef. Morgan assured them that he had not finished but would recess for lunch. After lunch he warmed to his topics and kept his oratory going all afternoon.

The shadows lengthened as the locusts and frogs began to call and the Republicans grew more and more furious. Just before the crowd was ready to stampede for home, Morgan expressed his regret that he had not had time to complete his explanation of the nation's problems but hoped he would have another opportunity. The crowd bolted, leaving the Republican arguments unspoken.

There is a strange coincidence in the fact that the distinguished careers of two men from Selma so closely duplicated each other. John Tyler Morgan served as a general in the Confederacy and had a long term as United States Senator—from 1877 until he died in 1907. Also from Selma, Edmund Winston Pettus entered Confederate service and rose to the rank of brigadier general. His career as a United States Senator covered twelve years, and he had just been reelected to the Senate when he died. Strangely, his death, too, came in 1907.

General James H. Lane of Auburn was known as the youngest general of the Confederacy.

General Joseph Wheeler led his Confederate cavalry so vigorously that he gained the nickname "Fighting Joe" Wheeler. During the Spanish American War, Wheeler again took up arms as a major general and led the cavalry division in the Battle of Santiago, Cuba.

William C. Oates was also a Confederate officer who became a brigadier general during the Spanish-American War, and this despite the fact that he had lost an arm during the Civil War.

One of Alabama's best-known military men was Colonel William Barrett Travis of Evergreen. He became a lawyer, but the brave battle of Texas to gain independence stirred him, and he joined Sam Houston's army. In February of 1836, Colonel Travis was in charge of the Texas forces at San Antonio when thousands of soldiers under Mexican General Santa Anna attacked.

Travis chose to defend an old roofless Texas mission, now known as the Alamo. He had less than two hundred men. When Santa Anna demanded their surrender, Travis wrote: "I shall never surrender or retreat. . .I am determined to sustain myself as long as possible and die like a soldier who never forgets what is due to his own honor and that of his country—victory or death." A hero's death did come to him and his companions at the Alamo.

INVENTIVE AND CREATIVE

Many inventors have been responsible for great creations but never received due credit for their work. Such a man was John Jonathan Pratt of Centre. The typewriter that he invented was described in detail in the magazine *Scientific American* for July 6, 1867. He had received an English patent for his invention but did not ask for an American patent until 1868. Earlier that year C. J. Sholes had received United States patents for a writing machine and Pratt received neither money nor fame for his pioneering work.

Dr. Luther L. Hill, father of Senator Lister Hill, was the first surgeon ever to perform a successful operation on the human heart.

Another notable Alabama medical man was Dr. Thomas Fearn, who advanced the treatment of malaria by using quinine.

Among the world's distinguished scientists the name of Dr. Robert J. Van de Graaff of Tuscaloosa ranks high. He developed the first machine ever to "smash" the atom. This high-voltage machine was called the Van de Graaff generator.

Any history of the space age would probably place at the head of the list the name of Dr. Wernher Von Braun, whose work did much to make Huntsville a rocket center.

The first writer of Alabama to be given general recognition was Octavia Walton Le Vert of Mobile, who wrote of the famous men and women she had met during her many travels. Another writer was Augusta Evans Wilson, whose novels were very popular.

Founder of an entire school of music—the blues—was W. C. Handy, the black man who composed the *St. Louis Blues* and many other works. Handy was born at Florence. Another Alabama black man, William Levi Dawson, was the composer of a different type of music. Among his works is *Negro Folk Symphony*. Pattie Malone was born a slave near Athens. A splendid contralto voice brought her an international reputation.

In a highly specialized field of music, Sigmund Slesinger gained lasting fame. His principal accomplishment was the arrangement of music for the Reformed Jewish congregations.

Frederick Arthur Bridgeman of Tuskegee is probably the most widely recognized artist of Alabama. His work is owned by some of the world's finest museums, including the Corcoran Gallery of Washington, the Art Institute of Chicago, the Brooklyn Museum of New York, and leading European museums.

Nichola Marschall was a talented portrait painter but probably is better known today as the designer of the Confederate flag and uniform.

An excellent series of Alabama pictures was a group of fifty-four works on Birmingham steel mills done by artist Roderick Dempster Mackenzie. It is said that chemists can analyze the chemicals in the blast furnaces by the precise colors of flames that Mackenzie used in these paintings.

Charles Bird King's 1828 painting of Sequoya (George Gist), the Cherokee scholar who developed an alphabet and numbering system so that the Cherokee language could be written

SUCH INTERESTING PEOPLE

Many interesting Indian personalities have been associated with Alabama.

A peaceful leader and a remarkable man was the Cherokee scholar George Gist, better known as Sequoya. In 1800 he moved to Wills Town near Fort Payne and carried on the fur-trading business started by his mother. Here he did much of the work that made him famous. Without any formal training, with extraordinary patience over many years, Sequoya developed an alphabet and numbering system so that the Cherokee language could be written. The system was so easy that within a few years most of the Cherokee people could read and write. Sequoya's life and varied career made him one of America's great Indian leaders.

One of the notable and tragic American Indian fighters was Osceola, born in Alabama near Fort Decatur. He fought and died in the Seminole war in Florida.

Alexander McGillivray was the son of Lachlan and Sehoy McGillivray. Lachlan was Scottish and Sehoy was part Creek Indian. Through his mother, Alexander McGillivray inherited leadership in the Wind Clan of the Creek Confederacy.

Lachlan McGillivray was loyal to Britain during the American Revolution, and his property was seized. Alexander stayed among the Creek, became a British colonel, and helped many Tories. After the war he kept his English commission as superintendent general of the Creek nation but also received a Spanish colonel's commission, playing one side against the other. He then managed to persuade President George Washington to make him an American general, and thus held the commissions of three governments.

This powerful and crafty leader was a master of intrigue. Each country tried to win the good will of the powerful Creek nation through the Creek leader. In this way McGillivray won many advantages for his people.

David MacNac, also of Indian and Caucasian ancestry, was the first Alabamian to graduate from West Point. He was killed in the Seminole wars. The Indians had such a hatred for persons of mixed blood who fought against them that they filled his body with sixty-seven bullets.

Another military man is Marine Clifton Curtis Williams, a native of Mobile and the first astronaut from Alabama.

One of the Alabama's leading industrialists was William P. Lay, who came to Gadsden at the age of twenty-one. He became one of the principal figures in developing electric power for the South.

A modern-day Birmingham business leader with an interesting career is Dr. Arthur G. Gaston, a black man who began as a $3.10 per day laborer and rose to become the millionaire owner of a business empire in insurance, finance, real estate, and other fields.

Jesse Owens of Decatur gained his greatest fame in the 1936 Olympic games at Berlin, where he won the 100-meter race and set new records in the 200-meter race and the broad jump. Many felt a particular satisfaction that an American black man excelled in Berlin, where Adolf Hitler was calling his German version of the white race superior to all others.

Other Alabamians who gained fame abroad were Hoyt Smith De Fries, born near Oxford, and Grace Hinds of Decatur. De Fries became one of Queen Victoria's advisors in affairs of state, and Grace Hinds became Lady Curzon, Marchioness of Kedleston.

62

Teaching and Learning

Alabama as a state was only two years old when the state legislature passed an act that incorporated the state university. A tract of more than 46,000 acres (over 18,000 hectares) of state land had been sold for this purpose, and the proceeds deposited in the state bank. Construction was begun at Tuscaloosa in 1827, and the university commenced its classes in 1831 under the presidency of the Reverend Alva Woods.

There were only thirty-eight pupils in 1837 when the Reverend Basil Manly took over as president. Because he spied on the students and kept overly severe discipline even for those days, the students rebelled. There were protest marches and demonstrations until the rules were changed.

The state bank failed in 1843, and the university lost most of its funds. The Civil War brought many changes to the university, including the training of cadets for the Confederate Army. Many civilian activities were suspended, but the university was not closed until almost the end of the war, in April, 1865, as the result of the burning of most of the buildings. Only four years later, the university managed to reopen and has continued ever since.

One of the unusual distinctions claimed by the university in its history is the granting of "the first diploma ever issued to a woman by any chartered institution authorized to confer degrees."

Today the principal schools on the more than 400-acre (about 162-hectare) campus are Commerce and Business Administration, Home Economics, Law, Nursing, and the Graduate School. There are fine divisions of Arts and Sciences, Education, Engineering, and Chemistry. A medical center in Birmingham and research institute at Huntsville also are operated by the university. Total enrollment is now over 35,000.

To sports' lovers of the country, the phrase Crimson Tide means football. Alabama's famed football team usually holds one of the top ranks in the country, and its fans are among the most loyal anywhere. The University of Alabama has played in more post-season bowl games than any other team in the United States.

Above: Morton Hall at the University of Alabama in Huntsville
Below: The Administration Building at the University of North Alabama in Florence

Auburn began in 1872 as the State Agricultural and Mechanical College. Many felt that teaching such practical subjects was a mistake in higher education. However, the college provided expert professors in engineering and agriculture and graduated students with degrees in both subjects. It was one of the institutions to operate under the federal land-grant act.

Auburn was the first school in the South to have a department of electrical engineering.

In 1892, women were admitted at Auburn—the first time they had ever been given equal status with men in an Alabama college. The legislature changed the name to Alabama Polytechnic Institute in 1899, but the institution was always known by the popular name of Auburn University, and the name was changed to this officially in 1960.

Auburn is also noted for its football team—the Tigers of the Plains.

In order to give greater opportunity for girls to have technical training, Alabama's famed educator Julia S. Tutwiler led a movement that resulted in the Girls' Industrial School at Montevallo. Founded in 1895, and once called Alabama College, this is now named the University of Montevallo.

Birmingham leads the state in the number of educational institutions. The area offers six colleges, including the University of Alabama's Medical and Dental colleges.

The beginnings of Samford University go back to 1842, as Howard College in Marion. The Baptist institution now at Birmingham serves more than three thousand students on a 400-acre (162-hectare) campus. The School of Pharmacy is one of the largest and most highly rated in the country. Cumberland Law School, now a part of Samford University, has an outstanding reputation. Another Birmingham school with denominational ties is Birmingham Southern, a Methodist liberal arts school, founded in 1856. It is especially well known for its full program of adult education offered for the community.

Miles College of Liberal Arts is another Birmingham educational institution.

Tuskegee Institute found its beginning in the vision of Lewis Adams, who was once a slave, and who could see the benefits of technical education for people of his race. He was able to persuade both Northerners and Southerners to provide funds, and Tuskegee Normal and Industrial Institute was opened on July 4, 1881. Its thirty students were housed in an ancient frame building. Governor Rufus Wills Cobb was one of the sponsors of the action of the legislature chartering the institute.

Possibly the greatest asset in the early days of the institute was the fact that its founders had been able to persuade Booker T. Washington to come to Tuskegee as its head. He was a young educator who already had gained a reputation as an educational leader.

Throughout much of its history, Tuskegee Institute has concentrated on providing instruction in almost 50 trades and vocations. Today more than 3,000 students have the facilities of a 5,000-acre (about 2,000-hectare) campus with 150 buildings.

The Tuskegee Choir has long been known for its outstanding vocal presentations.

Other colleges and universities include University of South Alabama and Spring Hill College, Mobile; Athens College; Saint Bernard, Cullman; the University of North Alabama, (formerly Florence State College), Florence; Judson at Marion; Huntington College and Alabama State, Montgomery; Talladega College; Troy State University; Stillman College, Tuscaloosa; Jacksonville University; Livingston State College; Oakwood College, Huntsville; and numerous junior colleges.

Alabama's first known school was founded in 1799 on Lake Tensaw by John Pierce, who was a cotton operator in the area. In a log cabin furnished with log benches, Pierce taught the children of wealthy families in the neighborhood. The ''blab'' method was used for instruction. All the students read their lessons aloud at the same time. Although the quality of such education was not high, Pierce is said to have made a good profit from his school.

The first state legislature passed school laws and set aside property to support schools. Other laws were passed as the years went by, but a statewide educational program was slow in developing.

Silsby Science Hall and Swayne Hall, two of the buildings on the Talladega College campus

Mobile established a system of education in 1852. It was so successful that in 1854 a state system of education based on the Mobile plan was devised. The system gave counties power to tax real estate and personal property for school use. The office of State Superintendent of Schools was also created.

In 1974, 764,000 students were attending the public schools of Alabama, taught by a total of 36,920 teachers.

One of the most interesting modern developments in Alabama's education is the Department of Education's Trade and Industrial Education Service. Intensive training for specific jobs is given at all of the eleven state trade schools to workers who are on a trainee's wage. If a new business firm opens with partially trained workers, a program is available to provide supplementary instruction by teachers who are craftsmen in their trades. There is also special state training for supervisory workers.

Enchantment of Alabama

Not long ago travel writers were invited to a tour of Alabama to learn about the attraction of the state. One of them expressed his amazement, "I had no idea Alabama had so much to offer. We have wafted over blue Gulf waters, rustled through venerable historic rooms, lilted across pine-ringed lakes, heard our voices echoed from picturesque mountain tops and resounded through mammoth caverns. We have been transported from the historical lands of the Indians, the Spanish, the French, the English to the roar of the space age, and we had them all and much more in star-studded Alabama."

MOBILE

Nothing quite like it had ever been seen before; Thor threw his thunderbolts; Zeus glowered from his chariot; Venus rose once more from the sea; Bacchus reeled down the street. Once more Mobile contributed to the world's festivities with a new idea.

The year was 1840, and the occasion was Mardi Gras, during which the first parade with a theme and title was held in Mobile. The colorful and lively affair was devoted to "heathen gods and goddesses." It was appropriate that this new feature of a theme parade with floats, which was quickly imitated by New Orleans and other cities, should have started in Mobile, for the Mobile area held the first Mardi Gras celebration in the New World in 1704.

The general form of Mardi Gras as it is celebrated today was pioneered by Mobile's Michael Krafft. In 1830 young Krafft gathered with a half dozen or so of his friends in Antonine La Tourette's cafe at the corner of Water and Conti streets. He suggested a parade from the cafe to celebrate the New Year. An unsteady but determined group trooped to Partridge's Hardware store at Commerce and St. Francis streets. There they gathered up an abundance of rakes, hoes, and cowbells; singing, shouting, waving rakes and hoes, and ringing the bells they paraded through the main streets and wound up at the home of Mayor John Stocking, Jr., who invited them in and served refreshments.

The next year Krafft and his friends organized the country's first "mystic" society, and in time many of the ideas were translated to the Mardi Gras celebration. Today Mobile celebrates for ten days with fifteen afternoon and evening parades, bells, and other Mardi Gras festivities.

Another of the country's best-known festivals was begun in 1929 by the Junior Chamber of Commerce of Mobile. The city had been cultivating its famed azaleas since 1754 when azaleas had first been brought from France by Fifise Langlois. As early as 1760 visitors came from as far as France to view the gorgeous flowers in Langlois' garden. The Jaycees organized a route over which visitors could go to see the most wonderful blossoms of the city and called it the Azalea Trail.

Today the Azalea Trail winds for thirty-five miles (fifty-six kilometers) past homes, parks, and gardens, which together make up America's most spectacular single floral display. Huge mounds of azaleas as much as thirty-five feet (nearly eleven meters) long and twelve feet (more than three meters) high splash their mountains of blooms across public parks and boulevard parkways. Owners of private homes spend large sums to make their yards and gardens better than those of their neighbors. Each year many householders plant as many new azaleas as space and funds will permit. Everyone, of course, has his own idea as to arrangement of the plants.

The result is a splash of reds, pinks, whites, peach, and other colors in an almost endless array of azaleas.

In 1958 the ingenious Mobile Jaycees organized America's Junior Miss Pageant as the climax of the Azalea Trail festivities. Today, many television viewers can watch as the country's outstanding high school beauty is selected in Mobile.

Among the notable houses of Mobile is Oakleigh, restored by the Historic Mobile Preservation Society. It stands on the crest of Simon Favre's old Spanish land grant, in a setting of live oaks and azaleas. The society has provided furnishings of the period before 1850, and the second floor has a museum that includes a Mardi Gras collection.

The battleship U. S. S. Alabama *rests at anchor in Mobile Bay.*

Another interesting building is Fort Conde-Charlotte House. This was built in 1820 on the foundations of the fort, which dated from the early Mobile area settlements. For a while the building served as a courthouse and jail and then became a residence. There are French, English, American, and Confederate rooms, representing the various periods of history.

One of the most unusual office buildings in the country is the Waterman Building in downtown Mobile. In its lobby a huge world globe revolves under a ceiling dome that shows the night sky at different periods. Around the lobby are several beautiful murals.

In Municipal Park on the shore of a lake is the Mobile Art Gallery. The Mobile Municipal Auditorium and Theater is a fine facility.

The Municipal Auditorium and Theater plus the Phoenix Fire Company are portions of the phenomenal restoration of downtown Mobile. On October 9, 1964, Mrs. Lyndon B. Johnson dedicated the restored Phoenix Fire Station as a museum, one of the central achievements of the restoration.

The battleship U. S. S. *Alabama* was launched in 1941. Its 16-inch guns boomed at Tarawa in World War II. It went on to outstanding service in the Marshalls, Hollandia, Marianas, Carolines, Philippines, and far-ranging Pacific raids. The 35,000-ton (31,751-metric ton) ship led the fleet into Tokyo Bay to end the war.

When it was announced that the Navy would scrap the historic ship, Governor George B. Wallace led a campaign to save it. The United States donated the ship to Alabama. The people of Alabama contributed $1,000,000 (including $100,000 from schoolchildren) to bring the ship 5,600 miles (about 9,000 kilometers) from Bremerton Naval Yard, Washington, to Mobile Bay and pay the expenses of setting it up near a 75-acre (about 30-hectare) park. There in Mobile Bay the great hulk rests at anchor, dedicated in 1965 as a shrine to the sacrifice and courage of Alabamians of World War II and Korea. Today young and old wander over the vast decks, marveling at a wonder of a bygone war.

Not far from the battleship is the Alabama Historama, a private museum with action dioramas showing the Fort Mims Massacre, Spanish Fort Battle, and Battle of Mobile Bay.

Present-day Mobile is busy with its bustling port, food processing, petroleum refining, paper making, textiles, woodworking, and other businesses. But it is not too busy to remember its historic past, with its pirates, battles and alarms, hoop-skirted gentlewomen leaning against wrought-iron balconies, and other memories of a stirring yesterday.

THE REST OF SOUTH ALABAMA

Probably the most beautiful garden in the United States is Bellingrath Gardens, south of Mobile, during the azalea season. On 800 acres (about 324 hectares) of natural woodland Mr. and Mrs. Walter D. Bellingrath employed the finest landscape artists to plan an oustanding garden and plant 250,000 azaleas in 200 varieties, as well as hosts of other blooming flowers and shrubs.

Since the Bellingraths' death, the gardens have been operated by the Bellingrath-Morse Foundation and are open to the public. When the azaleas are at their peak in early spring, the reflections of vast sweeps of color on blue lagoons and forest paths banked shoulder-high with striking color surround visitors with beauty. However, each season has its own attractions and appeal. The Bellingrath house is open to the public and contains many treasures of furniture and art objects.

Other notable gardens not far from Mobile are the Long Gardens, covering ten acres (about four hectares) of the Earle W. Long estate, and the Clarke Gardens.

Alabama has a short but interesting coastline. Gulf Shores stretches for thirty-two miles (about fifty-one kilometers) of white sand beach from Alabama Point on the east to Mobile Point on the west. Here the entrance to Mobile Bay was guarded by historic old Fort Morgan, now part of a state park. This point has been fortified since 1559, when the Spaniards put up a strong wall to protect themselves against the Indians.

The present Fort Morgan was built in the shape of a five-pointed star and was based on plans first made by Michelangelo. When Confederate forces at the fort used marine mines, then known as torpedoes, during the Confederate Battle of Mobile Bay, Admiral David Farragut gave his famous command, "Damn the torpedoes, full speed ahead!"

The fort was used militarily during the Spanish-American War and World Wars I and II. There is a museum at the fort.

Opposite Fort Morgan is Dauphin Island, the western tip of which is now Fort Gaines State Park. It is also a five-sided fort, captured by Farragut on August 23, 1864. A museum displays relics of the Confederacy.

Dauphin Island now is connected with the mainland by a causeway, Gordon Persons Overseas Highway, and is a popular resort. The first settlement in Alabama was made on the island, which has a wealth of history, as is the case with many areas along the entire shore of Mobile Bay.

At Brewton during the Creek War, part of Andrew Jackson's army escaped a Creek attack by pretending to camp, making dummies to look like sleeping soldiers, and concealing themselves in the underbush. When the Creek attacked, they were massacred. Brewton is the site of old Fort Crawford, established in 1818 as a protection from the Indians. It is today a center of woodworking and textile weaving, also the headquarters for the Escambia Experimental Forest. When Brewton gained the county seat of Escambia County, its rival Pollard sent a carload of stray cats to Brewton where they were pests for years.

Andalusia has textile mills, furniture, lumber, and box plants and is the nearest community to Conecuh National Forest.

The town of Enterprise has one of the world's most unusual monuments. It is probably the only community anywhere with a memorial to an agricultural pest. The town appeared to be doomed when the boll weevil almost destroyed the cotton industry, but the peanut crop that replaced cotton proved to be so much more profitable that the town erected a monument to the boll weevil "in appreciation of what it has done to herald prosperity."

Enterprise now has one of the country's largest peanut butter processing companies and ships vast quantities of peanut products.

Dothan is the largest community of southeast Alabama and the marketing center for the "Wiregrass" section. Its manufacturing plants turn out peanuts, lumber, and cotton products. Dothan holds an annual Peanut Festival in October.

Luverne was the home of a picturesque character known as Big Sam Dale. Among his other accomplishments, Dale carried the news to Andrew Jackson that the War of 1812 had been ended. This news did not reach Jackson until after the Battle of New Orleans. When Big Sam finally reached him, Jackson roared, "Too late! Washington is always too late!"

MONTGOMERY

Historic Montgomery became the capital of Alabama in 1847. On the sites of the Indian villages of Towassi and Econchati, Andrew Dexter built a town called New Philadelphia, and General John Scott built a town known as East Alabama. These towns, once fierce rivals, were consolidated in 1819 to form Montgomery.

The beautiful capitol building, rebuilt in 1851 after a fire, stands on what was once Goat Hill. The Confederate government was organized in the present Senate Chamber of the capitol, and few visitors leave without seeing the brass star that marks the spot of Jefferson Davis's inauguration as first and only President of the Confederacy. It was here that Davis and the assembled crowd were photographed in what is believed to be the first outdoor photograph taken in Alabama. The photographer was Archibald C. MacIntyre of Montgomery.

Alabama marble forms the columns and corridors of the building. The most impressive feature of the interior is the graceful twin spiral stairway, swinging upward with airy grace—without any visible means of support. The unique staircases were designed by Stephen D. Button, architect of the building. The eight murals inside the capitol dome and other art work illustrate Alabama's heritage.

On the north corner of the capitol grounds is the Confederate Monument, for which Jefferson Davis laid the cornerstone in 1886.

The two-story frame house occupied by Davis as the first White House of the Confederacy stands at Washington and Union streets. It was used by the Davis family for only three months. Now it is a museum with relics of the Confederacy.

Other notable buildings of Montgomery include the Lomax House, Murphy House, Teague House, St. John's Episcopal Church, and the Exchange Hotel, where Jefferson Davis greeted a

Alabama's Capitol Building in Montgomery

roaring crowd from the balcony when he came to Montgomery to become Confederate president. The present governor's mansion was built in 1829 and was purchased for the state during Governor James E. Folsom's administration. The State Coliseum is said to be the largest convention and exhibition area in the Southeast.

The Montgomery Museum of Fine Arts displays American portraits and other art works, a large collection of Indian materials, and other exhibits.

Chantilly Plantation House and Jasmine Hill Gardens are near Montgomery.

THE REST OF CENTRAL ALABAMA

Selma perches high on a bluff above the Alabama River. It remains a gracious city with much to remind the visitor of pre-Civil War times. As an arsenal of the Confederacy, it was a target for Union forces. When it fell in 1865, two thousand of General Nathan Bedford Forrest's men were captured, and the shipyards, powder works, iron rolling mill, and other important supply sources were destroyed. Selma is the home of Sturdivant Museum, a beautiful antebellum mansion now open to the public.

Today there are several small industries in the area, along with dairy farms, pecan orchards, and livestock.

Not far from Selma are a few crumbling remains of Alabama's first capital, Cahaba. After being almost ruined by a flood, Cahaba made a comeback and became one of the principal ports on the Alabama River. The war and another flood left it the ghost town it is today; there is not a complete building standing.

Tallassee stands near where the principal Indian town of Huiliwahli once was. There the Creek Confederation met to consider resolutions of war. When war was decided on, the red war club was sent from there to all parts of the Creek Confederacy.

Today Tuskegee Institute has five thousand acres of land (about two thousand hectares) and accommodates more than three thousand students. The George Washington Carver Museum displays the original laboratory where Carver and his students made their equipment from junkpile discards. In the museum, dioramas show the contribution of black people to civilization, and the museum has a notable collection of art from Africa. Windows of the chapel tell the history of the black man. Also on the campus is the Booker T. Washington Monument, showing the Institute's founder raising the "veil of ignorance" from the head of the emancipated black man.

Phenix City is a principal manufacturing community on the Chattahoochee River opposite Columbus, Georgia. The nine-foot (nearly three-meter) channel of the Chattahoochee places Phenix City in a location as a principal port. Since World War II, newer industries have been attracted, adding to the earlier brick making, cotton textiles, and paper products of the region.

Phenix City will probably be remembered as the host town to the countless soldiers trained at Fort Benning during World War II.

Opelika and Auburn are twin cities that blend together without a break. Auburn University now enrolls over 15,500 students, who bring the population of the twin cities to nearly 60,000.

Alexander City is the center for one of the state's finest inland water-recreation areas—Martin Lake. When the lake was formed by Martin Dam in 1926, it was the largest of its type. One of the newest industries in Alexander City is the building of mobile homes. Ornamental iron and textiles are also produced there.

Nearby is Horseshoe Bend National Military Park, the site where Andrew Jackson shattered the force of the Creek Confederacy during the Creek War. The events of those times are explained at the park's museum and visitor center.

The Choctaw Indian words *tusko loosa* meant "black warrior." Today that phrase has been applied both to be Black Warrior River and that river's principal town—Tuscaloosa.

As the capital of Alabama from 1826 to 1846, Tuscaloosa was a place of bright social life, centering around the wealthy planters and their many cultural activities. The community was almost destroyed by the Civil War, but many fine antebellum homes still stand, and agriculture and industry have returned to make this a prosperous city.

On the grounds of the University of Alabama at Tuscaloosa is the lovely old mansion of the president. During the Civil War the president's wife prevented the Union troops from burning it. The home of Dr. William C. Gorgas, who drove the mosquitoes from the Panama Canal Zone, is open on the campus, as is the Museum of Natural History. Still standing is the Little Round House, a sentry point where students were fired on by Union forces.

The Governor's Mansion, once the home of Governor Arthur P. Bagby, is now the University Club, combining membership of town and gown.

Near Tuscaloosa is Mound State Monument, preserving Alabama's largest collection of prehistoric mounds. A fine archaeological museum at the park shows the background of the Mound Builders.

NORTHERN ALABAMA

The Tri-Cities of Alabama are Florence, Sheffield, and Tuscumbia. Florence prides itself on having been the home of four governors and two admirals. In 1941 the largest aluminum plant in America was built there.

Sheffield received its first promotion from Andrew Jackson and went on to become a leading center of this thriving manufacturing region. The principal cause of the area's growth was the Tennessee Valley Authority (TVA). Wilson Dam of the TVA provides immense and inexpensive power for industry. It has the highest single lift lock in the world. Wilson Lake covers the river for more than fifteen miles (about twenty-four kilometers) to the base of Joe Wheeler Dam.

Tuscumbia was originally known as Big Spring because of the spring that generated 55 million gallons (more than 208 million liters) every day and is still to be seen in the center of town. In Tuscumbia there are many fine old houses, but the most interesting is Ivy Green, birthplace of Helen Keller, who lived triumphantly in spite of being blind and deaf. The pump where Helen mastered the first word she ever knew—"water"—is still to be seen, as well as many of her belongings. Each year at Tuscumbia in July and August the Pulitzer Prize play *The Miracle Worker* is given. This is based on Helen Keller's life story.

Amazing Huntsville, nicknamed Rocket City, is probably unlike any other city, combining the old with the most advanced. Here the Territory of Alabama was organized in 1819. Six govenors have called the city home.

One amusing sidelight in Huntsville history occurred after wealthy Samuel H. Moore's cow Lily Flag won first prize for butter at the 1893 Columbian Exposition in Chicago. Moore held a ball for Lily Flag in the ballroom of his home, built in 1850. Many prominent people from all over the country accepted Moore's invitation and were introduced to the bovine guest of honor.

At the George C. Marshall Space Flight Center in Huntsville, visitors gain an idea of what is going on in space by touring the Space Orientation Center. The history of rocketry is presented, along with exhibits of rockets and pictures of astronauts. Other exhibits display the work of the center which has created the giant Saturn rocket, made the first American satellites, provided for the first recovery of animal life, and flown the first rocket orbital flights.

President James Monroe chose Decatur as an acceptable site for a town in 1820. During the Civil War, the seesaw of battle left only five buildings standing in the entire town. Today Decatur is a center of the North Alabama recreation area; a port with a nine-foot (nearly three-meter) channel on the Tennessee River; a resort town on Wheeler Lake; and a growing manufacturing community.

Near Decatur is Moorseville, the first town to be incorporated in Alabama. Much of it is being restored as an example of life in the late 1700s. Also near Decatur is Wheeler National Wildlife Refuge.

Not far from Haleyville is one of the much-heralded wonders of Alabama—a fine natural bridge with an especially long arch. Near Moulton is Pioneer House Museum, an old log cabin furnished with household goods and implements that were used by pioneers.

Cullman was founded in 1873 by Colonel John G. Cullman, who hoped to build a colony with other German immigrants. By 1880 the population was 6,300. On St. Bernard College campus is the Ave Maria Grotto which has miniature reproductions of famous shrines and church buildings of the world. This shrine was built during a period of fifty years by lay-brother Joseph Zoettl. Near Cullman is William B. Bankhead National Forest which includes the Bee Branch Scenic Area of the Sipsey River. Here is one of Alabama's few remaining stands of virgin hardwood.

Near Springville are the Crystal Caverns.

Talladega was founded in 1834. Andrew Jackson won the first victory over the Creek Indians in the costly Creek War near Talladega. The city still preserves a number of splendid old homes and is a manufacturing center. The Alabama School for the Deaf and Blind and Talladega College are here, too.

A blast furnace was built at Anniston in 1863 to provide war materials for the Confederacy. After the war a city was founded by men of both the North and South. It was a model town, designed in part by architect Stanford White. The city's name came from Mrs. Anne Scott Tyler (Annie's Town), who was the wife of a company executive.

Anniston's Church of St. Michael and All Angels has been called one of the most beautiful in America. The Regar Memorial Museum of Natural History has one of the largest and finest collections of its kind in the country. Near the city is Anniston Army Depot, among the largest in the United States.

Near Heflin was the gold rush boom town of Edwardsville, center of the gold mining section of Alabama.

Nestled in the foothills of Lookout Mountain, Gadsden was founded in 1840. It was named for James Gadsden who was famed for his Gadsden Purchase in Arizona and New Mexico. Today the city is a center of steel manufacturing. Fabricated metal, rubber, electrical equipment, and electronic devices are also manufactured in Gadsden.

Gadsden gained world-wide attention through its unique service during the Viet Nam War. It became the first American city to build an entire new community to assist the people of South Viet Nam. One hundred new concrete block homes were constructed in Viet

Nam and occupied by refugees from the Viet Cong. Service-type buildings, including a school and dispensary, were also built. The whole community was built with contributions by citizens of Gadsden, Alabama. The new town was called Gadsden, Viet Nam.

Another of The Tennesse Valley ports is Guntersville, where a Cherokee village once stood. The Cherokee lived here even after it became Gunter's Landing, when the coming of steamboats created a boom town. Guntersville Dam, Guntersville Caverns, and Cathedral Caverns are attractions of the area. The entrance to Cathedral Caverns, 128 by 40 feet (39 by 12 meters), is thought to

Guntersville Dam

be the largest natural cave entrance in the world. The Caverns also have the world's largest stalagmite, two hundred feet (about sixty-one meters) in circumference and sixty feet (about eighteen meters) in height.

Near Fort Payne are Sequoyah Caverns, named for the great Indian scholar who lived at the Cherokee town of Wills Town near Fort Payne for a number of years. Also near Fort Payne is DeSoto State Park, known for its spectacular Little River Canyon, said to be the deepest east of the Rockies. Citadel Rocks are strange formations once used by the Indians for ceremonial pedestals.

Cathedral Caverns

Human beings lived at Russell Cave, near Bridgeport, as long as ten thousand years ago. Donated to the nation by the National Geographic Society, it is now a national monument.

BIRMINGHAM

Nothing like it had ever been tried before. Birmingham iron-workers gathered around the mold into which they had recently poured six tons (nearly five and a half metric tons) of iron from Birmingham ore. A gasp went up as the mold was removed; there lay a huge head, glaring up with stern and determined eye. Another mold uncovered a gigantic torso; fantastic arms came out of two other molds. From still others came enormous feet supporting massive legs.

Like a crew for Dr. Frankenstein, welders gathered and began to join the parts together to form a monster—the largest piece of iron ever cast. Designed by Italian sculpture Guiseppe Moretti, this was a statue of Vulcan, mythical god of metals and metalworking. It represented Birmingham at the 1904 World's Fair in St. Louis, was brought back to Birmingham, stored in the fairgrounds, and almost forgotten.

In 1936 civic leaders and clubs resurrected Vulcan and built a 124-foot (nearly thirty-eight-meter) pedestal for him on Red Mountain, which overlooks Birmingham. They raised his gigantic bulk of 120,000 pounds (54,431 kilograms), standing 55 feet (nearly 17 meters) high, to the spot where he now holds his torch aloft over the city. When his torch burns green, it tells everyone that there have been no traffic deaths in the "Magic City" area during a twenty-four-hour period. Red marks a traffic fatality. America's second largest statue, Vulcan is a symbol of the energy and industry of Birmingham.

In 1863 a small blast furnace was built in the valley to provide metal for Confederate rifles and cannonballs. The furnace was wrecked by Wilson's Raiders in 1865. Two railroads crossed in the valley in 1870, and Birmingham was born. Within a year's time the

Elyton Land Company had sold most of the lots in the more than four thousand acres (more than sixteen hundred hectares) it had bought. The land brought a fantastic profit. The boom was on.

Only two years later, in 1873, cholera struck the infant city, and the national depression nearly ended the community before it was well begun. In the midst of all this disaster, Finnish-born banker Charles Linn decided to build a grand and very expensive three-story brick bank building.

To celebrate the completion of "Linn's Folly," he sent out five hundred invitations for a Calico Ball. Men and women from all over the country came in formal clothes made of calico. The event was a great success, and Linn's optimism was so contagious that Birmingham revived quickly. In later years it went on to become Alabama's largest city, principal metal center of the South, and one of the leading industrial communities of the country.

Nowhere else in the world can iron ore, coal, and limestone, which are needed for steel manufacturing, be found in one region in such abundance. Iron and steel manufacturing soon became the leading industry of Birmingham and its industrial neighbors, such as Bessemer. The city took its name from England's leading industrial city; its nickname is "Pittsburgh of the South."

Today industry is not dependent solely on iron and steel. Hundreds of manufacturers produce thousands of items, which include everything from relishes to railway cars, bottle caps to bridges. As a striking example of the city's industrial know-how, the Rust Engineering Company of Birmingham produced the gigantic rocket arming tower at Cape Canaveral (formerly Cape Kennedy). Furniture, industrial safety equipment, chains, cast-iron pipe, chemicals, structural steel, air cleaners, builders' hardware, and dozens of other products are made in the factories of Birmingham.

The city also has an outstanding cultural and social life, going back to the famed Calico Ball. The Birmingham Festival of Arts is said to be the world's oldest continuing festival of the arts. It starts with the brilliant Beaux Arts Ball. After this, each day of the festival is packed with concerts, dramas, operas, and ballets; there are outstanding exhibits of painting, sculpture, and crafts.

The city's two-day Fourth of July celebration with concerts, military demonstrations, and other entertainment, is claimed to be the most extensive in the nation.

The Birmingham Civic Symphony was founded in 1933, and there is also a Civic Opera.

The Birmingham Museum of Art is outstanding. Its collections include the Rives group of art from Palestine, a Kress Collection of Renaissance art, Dutch paintings including a Rubens, as well as prints, bronzes, and porcelains.

Theater is represented in Birmingham by the Actors Theater, the Center Players, the Town and Gown Civic Theater, and the Valley Theater.

An unusual musical activity was held for years in Birmingham—the general convention of the Sacred Harp societies where hymns were sung, some of them dating back to the Reformation.

Birmingham people are also great sports enthusiasts. During the famed annual clash between Auburn University and the Crimson Tide of the University of Alabama, more than seventy thousand ardent fans pack themselves into Legion Field.

In the Birmingham Civic Center, buildings in Woodrow Wilson Park include the very modern City Hall, the Municipal Auditorium, the Public Library, the Chamber of Commerce Building, and the Jefferson County Courthouse, built in 1931.

Another interesting downtown building is the Liberty National Life Insurance Building, topped by the largest replica of the Statue of Liberty ever constructed—standing thirty-one feet (more than nine meters) high. Guides known as ''Liberty Belles'' conduct tours to view Miss Liberty.

Birmingham's Medical Center covers fifteen city blocks and contains more than thirty health-service facilities. Highly skilled medical personnel and specialized services draw patients from the entire Southeast as well as the entire nation. The Medical Center stresses a three-fold program of education, research, and community service. The Medical College of Alabama was founded in Mobile in 1859. Always a part of the University of Alabama, the Medical College was moved to the main campus in Tuscaloosa for some years before being reestablished in Birmingham. During World War II the Medical College was moved from Tuscaloosa to Birmingham. The University Hospital School of Nursing trains more than two hundred student nurses.

Southern Research Institute, one of the South's independent laboratories, has gained fame in the fields of cancer and industrial research.

Birmingham's Jimmy Morgan Zoo was not established until 1955. In the short time since, it has become one of the great zoos in the country, the youngest of them all. It is now the largest zoo in the nine-state area of the Southeast. In connection with the zoo are botanical gardens and a conservatory, both the largest in the South.

The only antebellum home in Birmingham is Arlington (open to the public) with its period furniture including many rare pieces.

One of the most unusual buildings in the Birmingham area was bought and is now occupied by the Vestavia Baptist Church. This was built as a home by former Mayor of Birmingham George B. Ward. He had architects make a copy of the circular, columned Temple of the Vestal Virgins in Rome. So today a Christian church occupies a temple of heathen Rome.

Unusual in an entirely different way is the fact that Birmingham is possibly the only major city to use two entirely separate water supply systems—one for industrial use and the other for domestic purposes.

Bessemer, another leading Alabama industrial city, and many suburbs such as beautiful Homewood and elegant Mountain Brook are attractions of the Birmingham area. Crystal Caverns, Rickwood Caverns, and Oak Mountain State Park are nearby natural features.

Of the many attractions of the region one is not so well known. This is another statue in Vulcan Park, also looking out over the city. It is the calm white marble likeness of the well-loved, almost legendary, Reverend James A. Bryan, for nearly fifty years pastor of the Third Presbyterian Church of Birmingham.

The statue was moved to a spot called Prayer Point in 1966; the placing of this statue so near to the giant figure representing industry perhaps also is symbolic—representing another phase of the spirit of Birmingham and Alabama as they look forward to the future.

86

Handy Reference Section

Instant Facts

Became the 22nd state, December 14, 1819
Capital—Montgomery, founded 1814
State motto—*Audemus jura nostra defendera* (We dare defend our rights)
Familiar name—Heart of Dixie
State bird—Yellowhammer
State fish—Tarpon
State tree—Southern Pine
State flower—Camellia
State song—*Alabama,* music by Edna Goeckel Gussen, words by Julia Tutwiler
Area—51,609 square miles (133,667 square kilometer)
Greatest length (north to south)—331 miles (533 kilometers)
Greatest width (east to west)—207 miles (333 kilometers)
Highest point—2,407 feet (734 meters), Cheaha Mountain
Lowest point—Sea level
Geographic center—Chilton, 12 miles (19 kilometers) southwest of Clanton
Highest recorded temperature—112° F. (44.4° C.), Centerville
Lowest recorded temperature— -24° F. (-31.1° C.), Russellville
Population—3,890,061 (1980 census)
Population density—75 persons per square mile (29 persons per square
                kilometer), 1980 census
Principal cities—Birmingham, 284,413
                Mobile, 200,452
                Huntsville, 142,513
                Montgomery, 178,157
                Tuscaloosa, 75,143
                Gadsden, 47,565
Number of cities over 10,000 population—40
Population rank in nation—22nd
Number of counties—67
Birthrate—17.6 per 1,000 people
Infant mortality rate—22.2 per 1,000 births
Physicians per 100,000 population—89
Acceptable hospital beds—4.2 per 1,000
Education expenditures—$217.54 per capita annually
Number enrolled in public schools—758,721

You Have a Date with History

1505—Mobile Bay shown on European maps
1519—Alonso Alvarez de Pinceda entered Mobile Bay
1528—Panfilo de Narvaez reaches Mobile Bay
1540—Hernando de Soto wreaks havoc
1558—Guido de las Bazáres explores Mobile Bay

1559—Tristán de Luna begins settlement, unsuccessful
1629—King of England grants much of region to Sir Robert Heath
1682—La Salle claims region for France
1702—Le Moyne brothers found Fort Louis de la Mobile at Twenty-Seven Mile Bluff
1704—Parish of Mobile organized
1711—Mobile established, rather than in 1710 as thought until recently
1714—Fort Toulouse set up near present Wetumpka
1719—First shipload of slaves brought in
1763—British take control
1780—Spanish Governor Bernardo Gálvez captures Mobile Bay
1783—Northern Alabama ceded to America by Great Britain
1798—Territory of Mississippi formed (included much of present Alabama)
1813—Creek War; General James Wilkinson captures Mobile
1814—Treaty of Fort Jackson ends Creek War
1817—Territory of Alabama organized
1818—Alabama's first iron furnace operates at Russellville
1819—Statehood
1826—Capital moved from Cahaba to Tuscaloosa
1830—First railroad west of Alleghenies chartered
1846—Montgomery becomes Capital
1861—Secession; Montgomery is Capital of Confederacy
1864—Farragut captures Mobile Bay
1865—Mobile, Selma, Tuscaloosa fall; war ends
1867—Federal forces place state under military rule
1868—Alabama readmitted to the Union
1871—Birmingham founded
1890—Making of iron and steel emerged as Alabama's chief industrial production
1901—New constitution ratified
1916—Muscle Shoals development authorized
1917—Seaman Kelly Ingram first Navy man killed in World War I
1923—State Dock Commission formed to create Port of Mobile
1929—Mobile Jaycees organize Azalea Trail
1932—Scottsboro case decided
1933—TVA comes into being
1936—Vulcan installed on Red Mountain at Birmingham
1941—World War II begins, in which 288,003 from Alabama serve
1949—Huntsville rocket projects are begun
1958—Explorer I, built at Huntsville, goes into orbit
1960—First Saturn rocket tested at Huntsville
1965—Battleship U. S. S. *Alabama* dedicated as shrine
1967—Lurleen Wallace takes oath as governor
1968—George Wallace runs for presidency on third-party ticket
1972—Governor George Wallace injured in assassination attempt
1974—George Wallace begins new term as governor
1983—George Wallace elected governor again

Thinkers, Doers, Fighters

People of renown who have been associated with Alabama

Bankhead, John H., Sr.
Bankhead, John H., Jr.
Bankhead, Tallulah Brockman, II
Bankhead, William B.
Bellingrath, Walter D.
Bridgeman, Arthur
Bryant, Paul (Bear)
Carver, George Washington
Davis, Jefferson
Gaston, A. G.
Gist, George (Sequoya)
Gorgas, William Crawford
Handy, W. C.
Hill, Lister
Hill, Luther L.
Jackson, Andrew
Keller, Helen Adams
King, William R.

Lay, William Patrick
Morgan, John Tyler
Osceola
Owens, Jesse
Owsley, Frank Lawrence
Pratt, John Jonathan
Rose, Frank Anthony
Semmes, Raphael
Sibert, William L.
Sparkman, John
Strode, Hudson
Travis, William Barrett
Van de Graaff, Robert J.
Von Braun, Wernher
Washington, Booker Taliaferro
Wheeler, Joseph (Fighting Joe)
Wilson, Augusta Evans

Annual Events

January—Senior Bowl Football Game, Mobile
February—Camellia Show, Birmingham
February—National Fields Trials, Union Springs
February-March—Mardi Gras, Mobile
February-March—Azalea Trail
March—America's Junior Miss Pageant, Mobile
March—Arts and Crafts Week, Fairhope
April-May—Festival of Arts, Birmingham
April—Confederate Memorial Day, statewide
May—Fishing Rodeo, Bay Minette
May—Art on the Rocks, Gadsden
May—Civitan Horse Show, Guntersville
May—Horse Show, Birmingham
May—Dixie Sailboat Regatta, Alexander City
May—Strawberry Festival, Cullman
June—Peach Festival, Clanton
June—Boat Race Festival, Guntersville

June—Outboard Races, Lake Jackson, Florala
June—Art on the Lake, Guntersville
June—Pleasure Boat Races, Smith Lake, Cullman
July—Fourth of July Celebration, Birmingham
July—Ski Races, Killen
July—Sailing Races, Point Clear
July—Sailboat, Slalom, Powerboat Races, Fairhope
July—Peach Festival, Chilton County
July—Handicap Boat Race, Martin Lake
July-August—*Miracle Worker,* play, Tuscumbia
July-August—Tennessee Walking Horse Show, Athens
July-August—Deep-sea Fishing Rodeo, Gulf of Mexico off Alabama
August—Blessing of the Shrimp Fleet, Dauphin Island
August—State Championship Rodeo, Athens
August—Motorboat Regatta, Guntersville
August—National Produce Festival, Fort Payne
August—Tri-Counties Fox Hunters Association, Fort Payne
August—Civitan Club Horse Show, Guntersville
August—Parade of Boats and Trawlers, Bayou La Batre
August—Southeastern Division Outboard Championship Races, Pell City
August—Alabama Deep-sea Fishing Rodeo, Dauphin Island
September—Manitou Cave Art Show, Fort Payne
September—Central Alabama Fair, Selma
September—North Alabama State Fair, Florence
October—State Fair, Birmingham
October—South Alabama Fair, Montgomery
October—National Peanut Festival, Dothan
October—Gulf States Fair, Mobile
October—Fall Sailing Festival and Races, Fairhope
November—Speckled Trout Rodeo, Gulf Shores
November—Peanut Festival, Dothan
December—Blue-Gray Football Game, Montgomery
December—Alabama Day, statewide

Governors of the State of Alabama

William Wyatt Bibb, 1819-1820
Thomas Bibb, 1820-1821
Israel Pickens, 1821-1825
John Murphy, 1825-1829
Gabriel Moore, 1829-1831
Samuel B. Moore, 1831
John Gayle, 1831-1835
Clement C. Clay, 1835-1837

Hugh McVay, 1837
Arthur Bagby, 1837-1841
Benjamin Fitzpatrick, 1841-1845
Joshua L. Martin, 1845-1847
Reuben Chapman, 1847-1849
Henry Watkins Collier, 1849-1853
John A. Winston, 1853-1857
Andrew Moore, 1857-1861

John Gill Shorter, 1861-1863
Thomas H. Watts, 1863-1865
Lewis Parsons, 1865
Robert M. Patton, 1865-1867
William H. Smith, 1868-1870
Robert Burns Lindsay, 1870-1872
Davis Lewis, 1872-1874
George Smith Houston, 1874-1878
Rufus W. Cobb, 1878-1882
Edward O'Neal, 1882-1886
Thomas Seay, 1886-1890
Thomas Goode Jones, 1890-1894
William C. Oates, 1894-1896
Joseph Forney Johnston, 1896-1900
William J. Samford, 1900-1901
William D. Jelks, 1901-1907
Braxton Bragg Comer, 1907-1911
Emmett O'Neal, 1911-1915

Charles Henderson, 1915-1919
Thomas Erby Kilby, 1919-1923
William W. Brandon, 1923-1927
Bibb Graves, 1927-1931
Benjamin M. Miller, 1931-1935
Bibb Graves, 1935-1939
Frank M. Dixon, 1939-1943
Chauncey Sparks, 1943-1947
James E. Folsom, 1947-1951
Gordon Persons, 1951-1955
James E. Folsom, 1955-1959
John M. Patterson, 1959-1963
George C. Wallace, 1963-1967
Lurleen Wallace, 1967-1968
Albert P. Brewer, 1968-1971
George C. Wallace, 1971-
George C. Wallace, 1971-1979
Forrest H. James, Jr. 1979-1983
George C. Wallace 1983-

Fort Morgan

Index

Italicized page numbers indicate illustrations

PICTURE CREDITS

Color photographs courtesy of the following: The State of Alabama Bureau of Publicity and Information, pages 12, 15, 38, 44, 47, 52, 75, and 91; The Alabama Development Office, 49; Library of Congress, 24, 33, and 61; USDI, EROS Space Survey, EROS Data Center, 4-5; The William Clements Library, University of Michigan, Ann Arbor, 8; Horseshoe Bend National Military Park, 27; Allan Carpenter, 41.

Illustrations on pages 17, 20, 54, 70, 82, and back cover by Tom Dunnington.

ABOUT THE AUTHOR

With the publication of his first book for school use when he was twenty, **Allan Carpenter** began a career as an author that has spanned more than 135 books. After teaching in the public schools of Des Moines, Mr. Carpenter began his career as an educational publisher at the age of twenty-one when he founded the magazine *Teachers Digest*. In the field of educational periodicals, he was responsible for many innovations. During his many years in publishing, he has perfected a highly organized approach to handling large volumes of factual material: after extensive traveling and having collected all possible materials, he systematically reviews and organizes everything. From his apartment high in Chicago's John Hancock Building, Allan recalls, "My collection and assimilation of materials on the states and countries began before the publication of my first book." Allan is the founder of Carpenter Publishing House and of Infordata International, Inc., publishers of *Issues in Education* and *Index to U. S. Government Periodicals*. When he is not writing or traveling, his principal avocation is music. He has been the principal bassist of many symphonies, and he managed the country's leading non-professional symphony for twenty-five years.